Barmaids, doctors, ta... 
spinsters, policemen a... 
rub shoulders with sha... ...ady
limericks in a brand ne... ...gn-in from
the publishers of *Rugby Songs* and
*Rugby Jokes*.

# Son of Rugby Jokes

SPHERE BOOKS LIMITED

First published in Great Britain by
Sphere Books Ltd 1970
27 Wright's Lane, London W8 5TZ
Reprinted 1970, 1973, 1976, 1978, 1979, 1981, 1984,
1985, 1986

PUBLISHERS' NOTE
No copyright is claimed for any of the stories in this book, nor
for the poem on page 151 ff marked with an asterisk.

All the limericks, and all the other poems have been specially
composed for this book, and should not be reproduced without
acknowledgement.

TRADE
MARK

Set in Monotype Baskerville

Printed and bound in Great Britain by
Collins, Glasgow

# SON OF RUGBY JOKES

# One With Whiskers On

An army officer who had been abroad for a long time, returned home to his wife. He had become used to high-class floozies in Japan, and was discontented because his wife would not shave her bush. She made all sorts of excuses, it was too cold in winter, it was shocking to her modesty, etc., and neither threats nor bribes would change her mind.

Her husband got fed up, and one night when he had been out with the Rugger Club boys for a drink, he decided to settle the matter. He carried his wife upstairs, threw her on the bed, and tied her hands and feet to the four corners with neckties.

She cried, she begged and she pleaded, but in vain. He plugged in his electric razor and was away. She told him he would regret it all the days of his life, but he scoffed at her suggestion.

As he finished and blew away the whiskers he found neatly tattooed underneath—KILROY WAS HERE.

## TOOK THE STUFFING OUT OF HER

A shapely girl was being forced to marry for money, a man she did not love. On the night before her wedding she decided to have one last wild fling with her former lover. He was not expecting her, and had not got a sheath.

In desperation they decided to use the skin of a saveloy, but owing to their passionate exertions, it came adrift, and could not be recovered.

On the wedding night she put up a very good show of violated innocence, but her rich middle-aged husband took his lust in five minutes and withdrew. He was amazed to find himself decorated with what looked like a sausage skin.

"I told you," she sobbed, "it's my maidenhead, and you've half killed me."

"Mary," he said, "I've seen a good many, but I never saw one with 'Marsh & Baxters' printed on it before."

# THAT SHOOK HIM!

There was a rich man's daughter who was rather plain, and in addition she had an unfortunate affliction—every time she got emotionally worked up, she developed a fearful fit of shuddering. Thus in spite of her money, she remained a virgin.

Along came a dashing young man who could charm the pants off any girl, and to the surprise of everyone, he married the rich man's daughter. Even more to the surprise of everyone, he seemed well content with his bargain, and as for the girl she purred like a pussy full of cream.

A famous doctor who had rather lost face by failing to cure the girl of her shakes, sent for the young husband, and said: "I've got one or two cases like this, a thousand quid if you'll tell me how you cured her?"

"Sorry, Doctor, but I haven't cured her."

"Then how do you account for your own satisfaction and the girl's manifest good health?"

"Hand over the money and I'll tell you."

The young man then explained that all he used was four neckties and a sharp penknife. "Good Lord! Go on."

"I take her to bed, and undress her. I kiss and fondle her, and she starts to shake. I lay her down and she begins to thrash about like a harpooned whale. Then I tie her hands and feet to the corners of the bed."

"Yes, and after that?"

"I get well in, then I cut the neckties, doctor, it's absolutely bloody fantastic!"

A man married a slut. She would neither keep the house clean nor get him a decent meal. She never took a bath, and he took to sleeping alone.

He got so fed up he asked an old friend what he could do, and the friend advised that the best plan would be to kill her with sex, which was not a capital offence. So the man went home one Friday, took a little food and wine into the bedroom, dragged his wife up and locked the door. On Monday morning he could hardly crawl to work.

He came home to find his wife in a spotless kitchen. She was stark naked, her quim shaved, her breasts reeked of eau de cologne, and she was cooking a splendid meal. . . . "You treat me right, darling, and I'll treat you right."

# THEN HER DRAWS CAME UP

There was a small boy who was caught by his father indulging in betting. This greatly upset father, who consulted the boy's teacher. She said the best thing would be for him to lose one really heavy bet, and get hurt, and that would cure him, and she promised father every cooperation.

That evening, when the class dismissed she told Johnnie to stay behind.

"I want to talk to you about wicked habits," she said.

"Ah," he replied, "and I want to talk to you Miss too, you're a cheat!"

This took her breath away, and Johnnie went on: "You pretend to be natural blonde, but you've got black hair between your legs—yah!"

"Indeed I haven't," she replied instinctively, before she fully grasped the enormity of what he'd said.

"I bet you ten shillings, two weeks' pocket money, you have," said the kid.

She'd landed herself in a trap, and anyway, she'd promised to help, there was no one around, so she took the bet. She dropped her knickers, lifted her skirt, and picked up the money.

She could hardly wait to dismiss the boy before phoning his father with the good news.

"Hell and damnation!" he said, "only this morning he bet me five pounds he'd see your quim before the day was out!"

# MEAT SAFE

The farmer was old, and his wife was young. To keep up with the work they set on a strong youth.

One day the farmer's wife went round the back of the barn and found the strong youth about to masturbate between two pieces of bullocks liver.

"Don't do that," she said, "there's a much better way, come with me and I'll show you."

"What about Maister?"

"Master's gone to market, come on upstairs." At which she got on the bed, took off her pants, and said: "Now put it in here."

"Both pieces Missus?"

There was a strapping young fellow who was on holiday alone in a strange town, and he thought he would go and watch some Club rugger on the Saturday.

The Secretary recognised him at once as a chap who had played scrum half for Northampton Town. "Look man," he said, "we've turned out a man short, the situation's desperate. PLEASE play for us."

The visitor explained that he hung up his boots when he had to have false teeth. The Secretary said this was only local Club stuff, several players wore dentures . . . the visitor looked, and it seemed to him that several of them wore crutches as well, and he allowed himself to be persuaded.

It turned out to be a hell of a rough match, and half way through the young man got a fearful kick in the mouth which broke his dentures to fragments.

He told the Club President that he had to return home that evening and lecture to Rotary, was there a chance of getting his teeth repaired, on a Saturday afternoon?

"Not a cat in hell's chance, but come home with me, I'll fix you."

* * *

An hour later he was drinking whisky in a very handsome lounge while his host kept trotting in with various sets of false teeth. . . . "Try these . . . now try these. . . ."

Some were too large, some too small, but at about the seventh go, they found a set of teeth that were near enough a perfect fit.

The young man shook hands and departed.

"It was vile luck to get my teeth shattered," he said, "but by the Lord Harry I could not have had a better break than to fall in with a dental surgeon, could I?"

"Dental Surgeon? Me? Not me, I'm a Funeral Undertaker."

The Royal Engineers were on a jungle exercise. They had to cross a raging river by means of a rope. The difficulty was to get the rope across, for the stream was wide and deep, and full of crocodiles.

The first volunteer to swim got eaten alive.

The crocodiles also got the second volunteer.

"Sapper Jones," yelled the Sergeant, "strip and swim with the line."

The Captain was aghast: "You can't send him to his death, he isn't even a volunteer!"

"Leave this to me, he's a Brummy football supporter, Sir."

By now, Sapper Jones was across, the crocodiles just sniffed and went away.

"Brummy football supporter! What the hell are you on about?"

The Sergeant said that if the Officer would go and look at the tattooing on the soldier's backside, he would understand everything.

On the left cheek he had: "Villa for the Cup," and on the right cheek: "Birmingham City League champions."

"Oh, I see what you mean, Sergeant, not even a crocodile could swallow that, hey?"

## ALL TASTES CATERED FOR

There was an oil rig in a vast and inhospitable desert. A visitor asked the Manager what on earth they did with themselves other than working. "Oh, we have lots of fun, let me see, today's Monday, when they fly the booze in. Would you like to stay for a blind-up?" The man said he was tee-total.

"Never mind," said the Manager, "hang on until Wednesday, that's when they fetch in the birds, lovely, young, coffee coloured. . . ." The visitor said he didn't like women.

"What are you then, are you a Queer?"

"No indeed I am not!"

"No, well in that case you'd better not be here on Saturday then."


## WHAT HAD SHE PRAYED FOR?

The Mother Superior had just concluded a prayer meeting in chapel to celebrate the forgiving of Sister Theresa who had been found in bed with a man. She went straight up to her cell and started to pack.

"What's the matter blessed mother?" asked the novice who was her personal maid.

"Matter!" she said, "I've been here fifteen years and three months. During all that time it's been penis and penance, fornicating and forgiving, well it's time for me to stop doing the forgiving and do some of the fornicating."

# A LITTLE FRICTION

Two old maids were getting neurotic, and consulted a doctor. He said, far better than cucumbers was a real man. He knew two students who were hard up, so had started a bull shop where frustrated women could go for treatment at a fee.

He gave the address, and off they trotted; on the way they passed a barber-shop, where the hairdresser was giving a customer a singe. There was a smell of burned hair in the air.

"Steady Mabel, I think we're walking too fast."

# THE RUB-OUT

A business man going to Japan was asked by a friend to bring back a parcel which could not be trusted to a shipping agent. When the man got back he was intrigued to know what could be in the large box, so he took it in the bedroom and carefully unwrapped it. It turned out to be a rubber woman, and he decided to give it a trial run. He inserted himself and touched a knob, which fell off, at which the thing went mad and began to suck him dry. He shouted to his wife, and gasped that he could not stop it.

She was a woman of resource, and cabled Japan: RUBBER WOMAN WEARING OUT MY HUSBAND HOW DO YOU STOP IT QUESTION MARK.

The reply came back: ORDER FUNERAL LADY WOUND UP ONE MONTH FOR WEST END BROTHEL.

# THE NAKED TRUTH

The local paper had been dropping some pretty hot hints about the conduct of the Lord Mayor and his sexy secretary.

Finally, a lawyer's letter was sent, and the paper promised to print a bold statement, clearing the matter up. There followed a headline:

THERE IS NOTHING BETWEEN THE LORD MAYOR AND HIS SECRETARY.

The Lord Mayor's lawyer rang up the Editor and said this wouldn't do, it could be taken two ways, next week's edition would have to put the matter clear beyond doubt.

All this time the Editor had been playing for time; he wanted to get enough on the Lord Mayor to be able to defend a libel action, and now he had got it. Therefore he gladly promised to put his meaning beyond doubt. The next edition came out with:

NOT EVEN A SHEET.

# FED UP

A machine operator in a newspaper printing office was getting married. The mechanics worked evenings in their own time to build him a splendid double bed with spring mattress.

After a few days he brought it back.

"What's the matter?" enquired the foreman, "aint it good enough?"

"No, just a question of adjustment gaffer, it feeds too fast!"

# THE GROANGREASER AND THE VIRGINS

Two old maids went out shopping, and, entering the greengrocers, enquired the price of cucumbers. The shopkeeper said: "Tenpence each, but you can have three for two shillings, it's a better bargain."

They looked at each other?

"Come on, Veronica, we can always eat the other one."

# IN THE PINK

A snobbish young woman did a great deal of hunting and horse riding, for her family kept a high-class hiring stable, with provision for little children as well. However, after a row with her parents she went off to London, determined to get work as a model.

She finished up with a top photographer who told her to strip off, and then, gazing with interest, said:

"You've certainly got rosy cheeks."

"Yes," she said. "I get those from horse-riding."

"So I see. You've certainly got the tits for modelling, but what about your ass?"

"Oh daddy will take care of that, it only needs stuffing with hay and a going over occasionally with a good stiff brush."


# NO BOTTLE

A woman went to a doctor with a bottle of urine, and said:

"My husband wants you to prescribe some medicine for his stomach pains, and he's too busy to come himself, so he's sent this."

The doctor emptied out the bottle, peed into it himself, and said:

"I believe your husband is a tailor. Take this and tell him to cut a suit to fit me, if he succeeds just by looking at it, I will do the same for him."


# SILLY ASS

A grumpy customer was playing up the waitress. "Would he like some oxtail?" "Don't be disgusting, Miss, I know where it comes from."

"Would he like some tongue?"

"I don't want anything that's been in an animal's mouth!"

"Yes, Sir, can I get you an egg."

## TWO FAST WOMEN

Two girls were driving through the pouring rain, and they were late for a date.

"Go on Mary," says the passenger, "put your foot down!"

"No fear," said the other girl, "we couldn't hope to buy off any speed-cops with the grass this wet."


## WHERE HAVE ALL THE YOUNG GIRLS GONE

There was a fourteen-year-old girl who developed a splendid figure, and she began to take a real interest in the lads.

Mother said to father: "You know, Dad, I'm getting very worried about our Mary, she spends too much time in the churchyard with the boys."

"Girls will be girls," said the old man, "you did at her age."

"Yes, but I didn't come home with my knickers starched and a shilling's worth of coppers!"

"Is that all? It could be worse."

"It is. Yesterday I found 'In Loving Memory' imprinted on the back of her best school coat."


## STANDING INSTRUCTION

There was a respectable businessman and Sunday-school teacher who liked to fill the house with "improving" texts.

One day the maid said to the mistress of the house: "I want to put my notice in."

"Why, Mary, you've always had a good place here, and been treated well."

"Yes, madam, but you don't know what the master's been up to in my bedroom."

The woman paled, steeled herself, and said: "What has he done?"

"He's stuck up one of them cards!"

The mistress rushed upstairs and read: "Be Ye Prepared, For Ye Know Not At What Hour The Master Cometh."

## SUBJECT NORMAL

Two hotel chambermaids were talking when the bell rang, and one had to go up to the room of a commercial traveller. He laid her straight down on the bed, took his will and in less than five minutes she was back downstairs.

"What did he want?" said her mate.

"Do you know, I honestly don't know, I think he must have forgotten, himself."

## POETIC INJUSTICE

Three daughters were getting ready to go out after tea.

Mother: "Where are you off to?"

First daughter: "I'm going off with Neal for a ride and a meal."

Second daughter: "I'm meeting Mick to visit a flick."

Third daughter: "I'm off with Hugh for a ..."

Mother: "Oh no you're not!"

## ONE TRACK MIND

Three women with young children went to a psychiatrist for advice.

To the first he said: "You've got a fixation on drinking, you even called your child 'Sherry'."

To the second he said: "All you think about is your stomach, you even called your little girl 'Candy'."

The third woman said: "I must go, I'm not staying to listen to this."

"I know where you're going too, you're going to meet your son Dick out from school."

## LONG TIME COMING

A girl was asked by her mother: "When you got home last night you stayed a long time downstairs with your boy-friend, I want an explanation."

"Oh Mother, if a boy takes you to the cinema you've got to kiss him goodnight for it afterwards, haven't you?"

"The pictures! I thought he was taking you to a very expensive night club?"

"Yes, Mother, he did."


## SINGLE MINDED

A newly married couple were in the back of a taxi on the way to the station. The groom interfered with her blouse, but she fought him off. He tried again up her leg. She turned to him angrily and said:

"Hey, lay off that stuff will you, don't forget, I'm a res-pectable married woman now."


## DUSTY ANSWER

A little girl came home, and asked her mother:

"Mummy, are dustmen religious?"

"I never thought so, why do you ask dear?"

"Well, this man emptied a full bin into the cart and he didn't see the other man, and he tipped it all over him and he just stood up and told God all about it."

The same little girl was too much under her mother's feet, so she was given the money to go to the pictures, a treat she had never previously enjoyed. When she came home, mother said: "How did you get on dear?"

"Well mummy, it was a bit like Sunday School."

"Like Sunday School, what do you mean?"

"Well, at Sunday School they sing 'Stand Up Stand Up For Jesus' and in the pictures they shout 'For Christ's Sake Sit Down'."

# PANNED

There was a girl had her eye on this chap, and she wangled it for her parents to be out when he called. She took him in the front room, turned up the gas fire, turned out the light, poured him a drink, and sat with him on the sofa.

She thought he would be slow, but he proceeded with every confidence. He stroked her hair, kissed her neck, then her lips. He crushed her to him, he pressed her back, he laid her down, he lay on top of her . . . then he stopped.

"Go on, go on," she moaned, "don't stop now or I shall die."

"But dearest, I don't know what to do next."

"You don't know what to do next you nit, what DO you mean?"

"Well darling, the pictures always fade out at this point."

# A BRUSH WITH THE FOREMAN

A young and innocent schoolgirl left and went to work in a broom factory. She worked well, and the foreman was annoyed when she gave her notice in.

"What's the matter, you're on good bonus, and doing well?"

"Oh no gaffer, I'm not stopping in this place, I'm catching a horrible complaint, it's all the stuff you use here, it's not nice."

After a lot of questioning he got her to say what the trouble was, since handling all these bristles, a lot of black hairs had grown between her legs, where all was bare before. The foreman explained that this happened to everybody, as they grew up, but she would not believe it.

Finally he took her into the Rest Room, dropped his trousers, and said: "Look here then what did I tell you?"

"Oh dear, it's worse than I thought," said the girl, "you've grown the broom handle as well."

## EXPANDING TRADE

In the old days, in East London, of a Saturday night, the butchers' and fishmongers' stocks would be laid out next the pavement on open slabs. The poorer women would come along looking for "bargains" and the tradespeople had a line of sales patter, and patience, up to a point.

But this woman hovered around, buying nothing. She picked up one bit of meat, put it down, poked it, picked it up again. . . .

Finally the butcher shouted: "Nah then Missus, taint like yer old man's yer know, gets bigger as yer play wiv it!"

## NOT LEGITIMATE

There was a certain boy, who, every Friday night of his life, had to go across town to his father. The father would hand the boy the affiliation money, which the boy took back to his mother. This had been going since sixteen years before, when the mother had obtained a Bastardy Order against the man.

One day the father said to the boy: "You're 16 today, is that right?"

"Yes, Dad, I am."

"Right, here's the last payment, here's a quid for yourself, now go back and tell your mother, I'm not your father any more."

"Yes, Dad, she told me to tell you, you never were."

# FOXS OFF!

A retired Ironmonger wanted to join the gentry, and he sent such large contributions to the hunt, that they felt they must let him join.

After the first "Meet" the MoF took the man on one side, and said:

"Look here, Bloggs old boy, d'you mind if I give you a hint?"

"I ain't bleedin' fussy, say what yer likes."

"Well old man, it is customary, when the fox is sighted, to shout 'Tally Ho!', not 'Get cracking you lousy buggers, there the little bleeder goes!'"

# TRUNK CALL

An optimist and a pessimist were in Trafalgar Square, watching a political demonstration.

Said the pessimist: "I bet I get crapped on by a pigeon."

Said the optimist: "Nonsense, there are ten thousand other people here."

The man WAS bombed by a pigeon, and he said: "Go on, you daft sod, tell me just one thing to be optimistic about, go on, just tell me, while I ruin my best handkerchief by wiping my hat with it."

"Indeed," said his friend, "let us be grateful that elephants can't fly."

# A BRUSH WITH THE LAW

A man went to the Health Insurance Offices and said he wanted a new National Health wig.

"What have you done with your old one?"

"I lost it."

"When?"

"Three months ago."

When they asked him why he had not reported the loss sooner, he said it was because he had been in jail.

They then asked whether he searched for it when he first lost it. . . . "Because unless you can prove you searched diligently, you don't get a replacement."

"Diligently! Listen! I was sitting in the cinema next to a girl in a mini-skirt when I lost it. Cor, diligently! I was groping around in the dark, and I could swear I had my hand on it twice. That's how I finished up in jail."

# HE WAS ON THE BOX

There was a notable rugby player who was about to get married. The boys advised him to lay off the game and save his strength, but he was too keen. The afternoon before his wedding he turned out for the Club, and, alas, got a fearful kick in the groin, and was taken to hospital where his member was put in splints.

After the wedding, when he and his new bride got to their hotel, and retired to bed, she was coyly undressing. . . .

"Look," she said, showing her breasts and quim, "untouched by man, these goods have never been unwrapped before."

"Don't you worry," said he, "mine's still in the box, as well."

# HE BOPPED A DROLLOCK!

Doctor Spooner, Warden of New College, used to live at famous Boar's Hill, Oxford. But he moved to the Marston Ferry Road, and when asked why, said:

"Ah well you know, I got tired of running up the whore's bill, I thought it would be cheaper to move to the fast and merry road."

Doctor Spooner got into serious trouble in Blackwell's bookshop whilst trying to purchase copies of *A Tale of Two Cities* and *Friar Tuck*. Until the dust settled, he moved to Cambridge, and greatly shocked a Dean's wife when he told her that his favourite inn was the "Fish and Duck".

# ALL BULL

There was a rough workingman who had been "signing on" at the Labour Exchange for all too long. One day the clerk asked him if he'd like a job abroad.

"What sort of a job?"

The man said it was rather a "blind date". All he knew was, it was for one of those rich oil magnates in Arabia. There was a book of travel vouchers, £50 in advance of wages. . . .

The labourer said, "Oh alright, he'd try anything once."

When he got there he was met by a Sultan's private physician, who said:

"My master wishes fifty maidens to be impregnated by an Englishman at five pounds apiece."

"Bloody hell!" said the man, "isn't that like Wolverhampton Labour Exchange to send a man all this way for two days' work?"

# A FELLOW FROM EALING?

Mae West was in her flat when three sailors arrived one after the other. Mae poured out drinks and said: "Only one of you can stay the night, we'll have to have a competition: I shall strip naked, the first man to pee on the floor can stay, the others must go."

Only one sailor could manage it, and he was disqualified for standing on his head.

# SOCIAL INTERCOURSE

There was a Debutante who married a Naval Officer, and he certainly knew his way about. He took her to Naples for their honeymoon.

When they awoke late on the first morning, they started again. . . .

"Dahlingest."

"Yes, Dahling?"

"Do the poo-ah do this, the proles?"

"Yes, Dahling."

"That should nevvah be allowed, it's much too good for them."

\* \* \*

After a week he said they'd better move on, he had heard that an earthquake was imminent.

"Yes, Dahling, but surely, those things are always confined to the poorah quarters of the town?"

\* \* \*

The Deb's sister wrote to her from America, where she had gone to try and improve the family fortunes. She said that already she had bought a new fur coat, and it only cost her a hundred bucks.

"She never could spell," said her sister.

# DEATH AND BENEFIT SOCIETY

Two Brummies met.

"Eh, Albert, is that right, you've joined the Conservative Club?"

"Ar, joined it last week!"

"But yo've allus bin a Labour man, all yower life."

"I know, but the doctor said I'd only got six months to live!"

"On'y got six months to live, wot the 'ells that got to you joining the Conservatives?"

"Well, I thought as how if any body'd got to lose a member it had better be them buggers."


# BLOODY IMPUDENCE

A Black Country chap said to his daughter: "I don't like that young chap as you're courtin', rough, and common, he is, and bloody stupid with it!"

"No, Dad, no!" replied the girl, "Albert's the cleverest chap I know."

"How d'yer mek that out?"

"Well, Dad, we've only bin courting nine weeks and already he's cured that little illness as I used to have every month."

# LIMERICKS I

There was a young lady named Muir
Perversion she would not endure
But opened her dimple
For sex pure and simple,
Saying: "Only the simple are pure."

As I went for my train to the station
My watch stopped, Oh Hell and damnation!
So I said to this dame:
"Have you got the time?"
She said: "Yes, and a strong inclination."

There was an old spinster named Flowers
Who watched the TV at all hours
She dreamed that "Night Rider"
Was in bed beside 'er
And stayed there for "Twenty-four Hours."

There were two young ladies named Feather
Who were feeling quite under the weather,
The Vicar, named Morgan,
Said: "Purchase an organ
And then you can play 'hims' together."

As this couple came out of a clutch
The kiss that she gave him was such
That he said to her: "Right
Are you free tonight?"
She said: "No, but I never charge much."

# Nudist "Camp"

There was a woman whose husband was a devil for the women. One day she told her best friend that the pair of them had joined a Nudist Club.

"Oh my dear, no! You don't mean to say you let him loose in that summer park, with all those woods and shrubberies; that you let him mix with big-breasted dollies, all starkers. You're asking for trouble."

"Not at all, we both love going there."

"But how can you take such risks? They say the wife is always last to learn, but surely you know what he is?"

"Of course, but you see, I always take jolly good care to decant him, immediately before we set out from home."

## LITTLE BIG HORN?

A rancher's daughter went for a long ride across the prairie, her horse fell and broke his leg, and she was very late back. Her anxious father looked out, and saw an Indian "whooo-ing" towards the ranch with the girl mounted up behind him. He gave the Indian a dollar, and said: "How did you manage to stay on, my dear?"

"Father, I nearly fell off, but he told me to reach round him and hang on to the saddle horn."

"Dern it! Don't you know Indians always ride bareback."

## THE SILLY ASS

It was a poor roadside cottage. The widow told her daughter who was doing the washing out at the front, that she must on no account take her hands out of the washtub as a regiment of soldiers were coming by. Moreover, she was not on any account to look round.

A number of soldiers, finding the girl's underclothes in rags, were able to take advantage of the opportunity presented. The girl said nothing for fear her mother should hear. The regimental mascot, a donkey, also saw his chance.

The girl said: "Will the last gentleman please leave his name and address?"

# OLD MARRIAGE CUSTOMS

A peasant youth from a mountain village in the Apennines went into the big city to work in hotels, and became educated by the chambermaids, who liked his rustic muscles and lack of inhibition.

He made enough money to go home and marry a virgin in the village.

On the wedding night he shaved off her pubic hair, took her in all three directions, smacked her behind with a hair brush, and finished up playing 69's. She started off objecting, but was very disconcerted to find that the longer it went on, the more she enjoyed it. She felt that this could not be right, and consulted the village priest, who, deeply shocked, immediately excommunicated the young man.

He took his new bride to New York, and a job at the Hotel Metropole. The local priest enquired why a good Italian boy was not coming to church. "It's a long story father, perhaps you could spare half an hour?"

"Tonight, at the presbytery," said the priest, "bring some whisky."

When the whisky, and the story were poured out, the New York priest laughed, and said: "That's all right my son, you're in again, don't worry."

"What father, no penances, nothing to pay?"

"Not a dime."

"But our village priest way back home said. . . ."

"Listen Alfonso, I don't want to denigrate my brothers, but really, what would a hick priest from the mountains be expected to know about normal modern western marriage customs."

# RUCKING THE DUCK

A society woman had a son of eighteen, and she was very worried about him, and went to consult a psychiatrist. "Tell me all about it," said he. The lady explained that the son had gone downstairs in the night, and eaten a duck out of the fridge. Then she had caught him masturbating . . .

"No harm so far," said the doctor.

". . . in the knickers of my thirteen-year-old niece!" She added that she thought the boy would have to be put in the looney-bin.

"Not at all," said the doctor, "had he masturbated in the duck, and eaten the young lady's knickers there would have been cause for concern, but up to now it's all been natural and normal."

# CAT CREPT IN CROFT

There was a clergyman in a tough district who was not satisfied with the behaviour of his congregation. The trouble was, they didn't believe in Hell Fire any more, so he decided to teach them a lesson.

He said to the Verger: "Listen, next Sunday morning I'm going to preach Hell Fire and damnation at this shower, I'm really going to get stuck into them and frighten the wit out of them."

He went on to explain that the Verger was to hide up in the rafters of the roof, armed with lots of bits of scrap paper. The parson would preach, and when he got to the line: "And fire rained down upon them" the Verger was to light the pieces of paper and float them down on the heads of the congregation.

Afterwards the parson would explain it was only a trick, but . . . "You never know."

The parson preached his heart out, he got them really worked up, and when he got to the payoff line: "And flames of fire rained down out the heavens upon them . . ." nothing happened.

This was appalling! He tried again: "And flames of fire rained. . . ."

There was a silence penetrated only by:

"It's no bloody use, Vicar, the cat's pissed on the matches."


# PART OF HIS EDUCATION

There was a new young priest went to his first parish, a mining village, and the old priest arranged to be in the back of the confessional, to see if the young beginner did it right. The young man tried hard, and afterwards said:

"I didn't do too badly, did I father?"

"Well, not too badly for the first time, but next time can we have a little less: 'Whew oo-oo-ew!' and a lot more 'Tut-tut-tut'?"

# WORTH PRAYING FOR

There was an Irishman visiting a strange town along with his English friend, and they were pretty bored in the evening. The Irishman decided to go to confession, and told the priest he'd been having sex with a girl.

The priest cross-examined him at length, but he wouldn't say who it was, so he got thrown out.

Waiting outside the church, his pal said: "Did you get absolution?"

"I damn well didn't, but I got some useful names and addresses."

# PUT HER FOOT IN IT

The Mother Superior of the Convent awoke in a particularly happy mood, dressed, and set off to visit her flock at their labours. The first nun she came to was Sister Theresa:

"Good morning, Sister, God bless you! Are you happy at your work?"

"Yes indeed, Reverend Mother, but I'm sorry to see that you got out of bed on the wrong side this morning."

The remark distressed the Reverend Mother, but she decided to ignore it, and passed on to where another nun was busy at her task. . . .

"Good morning, Sister Bridgid, you look pleased with yourself this lovely day."

"Indeed I am Reverend Mother, everything's all right with me, but it's a pity you got out of bed on the wrong side today!"

The Mother Superior, greatly puzzled, moved on to where a little novice was working:

"Before I wish you God's blessing and a happy day, little Sister, tell me something – do you get the impression I must have got out of bed on the wrong side?"

The nun blushed, hesitated, and said: "I'm afraid so, Reverend Mother!"

"And in the name of the holy Church, why do you all say that – am I not as happy as a songbird, and pleasant to you all?"

"Yes indeed Mother, but you see, er, but you see, you're wearing Father O'Connor's house slippers."

## TO THE POINT

There was a businessman who was middle-aged and not very prepossessing. He set on a typist of 18, and soon began to take her out to dine. However, he saw he was making no progress, so he started to buy her presents.

Asked what she wanted for her birthday, she said, "A real leopard-skin coat." This cost the earth, but he got her one.

One day in the office he said: "Joan, your knickers are coming down."

She blushed, hastily explored under her very short skirt, and said: "Oh no they're not."

"Yes they are, or else that coat goes back to the shop."


## SUPPLY AND DEMAND

A little boy and a little girl playing alone in a shed. They decide to take their clothes off, and little girl is very upset to see that little boy has got something she hasn't got. Little boy torments her about his superiority, and she runs home to Mammy, crying.

"What's the matter dear?" said Mother, "has Johnny been hitting you?"

"No," says little girl, pointing to her fanny, "but he's got something there that I haven't got."

"Don't worry my dear," says Mother, very relieved, "believe me darling, as long as you've got one of *these*, you'll always be able to get one of *those*."


## OLD CHINESE CUSTOM

Three Chinese girls discussing marriage. One said she hoped to marry a man of good birth, with two dragons on his shirt.

The next said she hoped to marry a man of good birth and great wealth, with three dragons on his shirt.

The third said she had no ambition for birth or wealth, she simply hoped to marry a man with one dragon on the floor.

# WHERE DID THAT SOD GO?

There was a peppery old Colonel went to play golf. The only other man waiting for a game was the newly appointed Bishop, so they introduced themselves and set off.

The Colonel drove a mighty drive, and removed a large divot, the ball remaining stationary.

"Bugger it, missed!" said he.

The Bishop was put out, and said so.

A bit further on the Colonel again foozled a shot, and hissed: "Bugger it, missed!"

At this point the Bishop really told him off about his language, and finished up: "I warn you, the Almighty is not mocked, if you come out with any more swearing, something dreadful will happen to you."

The Colonel kept himself under control, and, needing the last hole for the match, was left with a six-inch putt.

He took careful aim and . . . missed!

His flow of blasphemies was interrupted by a terrible clap of thunder, a flash of lightning came out of the sky, and struck the Bishop dead.

From behind a black cloud was heard a deep-throated rumble: "Bugger it, missed!"

# BALLS TO YOU, MISS

It was during the London air-raids, when many town children were evacuated to the country for the first time. A party of cockney kids were entering the hallway of a great manor. On the table was a brass dish, in which by chance there happened to be a couple of old golf balls.

"Wot's them rahnd things?" said a girl of twelve to the Squire's wife.

"They're golf balls my dear."

As everybody knows, the children drifted back, until the coming of the V-2 rockets, when there was another mass evacuation. . . .

The same child entered the same hallway, and this time there were four golf balls in the dish.

"Ah, missis, I see your old man's shot another golf."

# A REAL GENTLEMAN

There was a parson noted for good works amongst the poor. One day he was visited by a woman in distress. She was the most unpleasing female he had ever set eyes on, dirty, bedraggled and foul of breath. Her ragged blouse had no buttons, exposing shrivelled dugs beneath. He thought she was sixty, but it turned out she was forty-five.

She told a long tale of how her husband had run away and left her with ten children, and all the time she spoke the parson was hypnotised by her one tooth, a long black fang.

She wanted the Vicar to help her get the kids in an orphanage. He was kind, he was patient, and he explained that there were various funds which would help to keep the family together, rather than break it up. After a great deal of work he got her afloat again.

\* \* \*

Twelve months later the Vicar was in his study when his wife came in and said: "There's a fearful drab on the doorstep, and she must see you."

"Really," he said, "you know I'm writing my sermon, tell her to come back some other time."

"You're quite right dear," said his wife, "really, she's got one black tooth that. . . ."

"Oh her, she's a friend of mine, send her in at once."

The drab had come to explain that she was in trouble again – there was a new baby. The Vicar, who was a slow thinker, counted on his fingers, and said: "Here, your husband has been missing for 12 months!"

"I know," she said.

"Well, who is this man, the father? Is he going to pay you?"

"I don't know his name, Vicar, he was an Irish lodger I had, he only stayed two weeks."

*cont'd over*

"Good Lord in Heaven woman, you had all the troubles in the world already, what in the name of all that's holy possessed you to do a daft thing like this?"

"Well, Vicar, I thought it was very nice of him to ask me."

## OLD COUNTRY CUSTOM

An elderly landed gentlewoman was riding round her estates, with an old manservant in attendance. Away on a grassy bank she thought she saw something unusual.

"Heathers," she said, "What do you see over there?"

"A blanket, Madam."

"What is it doing over there, hey?"

"Moving up and down, Madam."

"Do you see anything else Heathers?"

"A pair of lady's legs wide apart, my lady."

"What else do you see?"

"A pair of gentleman's legs between them."

"And what do they think they're doing, hey?"

"Having intercourse, Madam."

"Good Lord, does that still go on?"

# DROPPED A CLANGER

There was a man went for a Government job, and when he was given a start the Labour Officer wanted his full name.

"What, just for a dockyard sweeper, my full name?"

"Yes my man, that is the strict rule."

The new sweeper was very shy about giving his full name, but at last said:

"All right then John Blast And Bugger It Smith."

Trying to keep a straight face, the Labour Officer said: "How did you come by that name?"

"Well, Sir, it was like this, just as the parson was christening me, some silly clot knocked the lid of the font on his foot."

# THOUGHT HE WAS NICKED

There was a youth in Ireland lived in the priest's house as his servant. As the boy grew towards 16 he began to feel certain urges, and asked if he could go to a dance. The priest explained that dancing meant moving around with young women in tight blouses, short skirts, etc. . . . in short, he was agen it.

The boy kept on so, that finally he was allowed to go to a dance at a town about six miles away, provided he got home by midnight. The dance finished very late, at two in the morning the frightened lad was creeping across the wild and lonely bog that led to his home. When he came to the "haunted rock" just as he feared, a dreadful creature jumped out. It had horns, and a tail, and flames were roaring out of its arse.

"Who are ye?" said the kid.

"I'm Old Nick, I'm the Devil himself," said the apparition.

"Och thank God for that, I was afraid you might be the priest!"

# THE HAYCOCK

It was the church outing, and they all picnicked on a farm. After the meal one young man climbed up a bank and lay down on his back on some hay, to rest. His girl came along, and said: "Let's make love." He said he was too tired, but she said, never mind, she'd do all the work. With which she slipped her pants off, undid his trousers, and squatted across him. She heard someone scrambling up the bank, so quick as a flash, she covered him up with hay.

The Minister appeared, and said: "Oh Miss Molly, why are you sitting there like that?" She explained that her grandfather owned the farm, and when it came to her she would build a new barn over *there* (wriggling round). She would also chop down that spinney over *there* (wriggling round the other way). And when she married, she would build a little cottage over *there* (swinging round again) with a track running back to the main road over *there* (wriggle, wriggle). "Indeed, Minister, you won't recognise the place when I've finished with it."

"Perhaps not," said the Minister, but I'm sure I recognise that pair of boots sticking out of the hay, they belong to my son." "Yes, Father," said a muffled voice, "and thanks to your bloody interference she'll need to build a nursery and a pram shed."

## THE SPIRIT MOVED HIM

There was a parson, full of good works, who used to do much jail visiting. One day he called in the cell of an "old lag" and said could he do anything for the man.

The man said yes, he would like to be read to, from the bible, of course.

"What would you like me to read?"

"The 119th Psalm please parson."

"My goodness brother, that's the longest psalm in the whole bible."

"Nemmind parson, I likes it."

So the good man read it over to him, and when he had finished, the old rascal said please could he have the psalm read to him all over again.

The parson said: "Yes, of course, I take it you have found true religion at last brother?"

"Well, it's not exactly that, but you see, I haven't had a drink for three years, and the smell of your breath's doing me a power o' good."

## NOT IN COLDSTREAMS!

There was a strict wartime rule that water, especially hot water, was not to be wasted.

A sergeant of the Guards was taking a bath, and two ATS girls were caught peeping through a crack in the bath hut.

Put on a charge, they said it was in the course of duty.

"And what the hell d'you mean by that?"

"Sir, we wanted to see if he had more than five inches."

## AT COVENT GARDEN?

A lady of the town was up before the Bench, and was asked to declare her occupation, she said she was a "dealer".

"Hey, what's that?" said the Beak, unbelieving.

"Sir, I am an old-established street trader."

"I'm not having that either," said the Beak.

The Learned Clerk, who wanted to press on, said: "Leave it to me, Sir, we'll just put down that she's in the 'whole-sale' business."

## "MISS" UNDERSTANDING

Some troops were stationed in a remote part of the Western Desert. One day a Brigadier flew in on inspection. They tried to keep him away from a thorn thicket that lay on the edge of the camp, but he would not have it so, and forced his way into the small enclosure. In the middle was a scruffy female camel.

Very suspiciously he bawled: "What the hell's all this?"

The young Lieutenant in charge explained that the place was a terrible long way from any women, and this camel was kept for the use of the men when they got desperate. The C.O. said it was disgusting: "Get rid of the wretched animal at once."

It so happened that some time later the Brigadier was actually posted to that camp, and after a few weeks he sent for the Lieutenant and asked what had become of the camel.

"After you'd gone, Sir, we put it back in the thicket."

That night when all was still the sentry saw the Brigadier enter the thicket carrying a stool, on which he stood and began to have intercourse with the beast.

"Hi, Sir! You're making a terrible mistake, the camel is only for the troops to ride to the nearest town on."

# DOGGED DOES IT

A cowed little much-married man thought he would give his wife a birthday surprise by buying her a bra. He entered a ladies shop all flurried, but the girls took him in charge ... what colour? ... He settled for white. The price ... forty shillings ... very good.

All that remained was the size. He hadn't the faintest idea. "Now, Sir, can we say, a pair of melons? Coconuts? Grape fruit? Oranges?"

"No," he said, worried, "nothing like that."

"Come on, Sir, think! There must be something your wife's bust resembles." He thought long and earnestly, then looked up, and said:

"Have you ever seen a spaniel's ears?"

A Stockbrokers Clerk of Ostend
Whose wife caught him bulling her friend
(And cried: "I can't bear it
Why shouldn't we share it?")
Said: "I never withdraw till I spend."

There was an old spinster named Mead
Who was prudish in thought word and deed,
Yet held it no scandal
To press on the handle
Of the vessel in which she wee-weed.

There was a young Scottie named Brown
Who offered a tart half a crown,
"We Campbells," she cried,
"Have still got our pride,
I'll never take that lying down."

There was a Director named Mitty
Whose blonde was all bottom and titty,
To his wife, he said: "Dear
I'll be latish, I fear,
I've a fair bit to do in the city."

A dropout and wastrel named Humming,
Did nothing but scrounging and bumming,
When his mother one day
Caught him having a lay,
He said: "I am now up and coming."

# As the Bishop said to the Actress

*As the Bishop said to the Actress:*
I'll try and come more often. . . .

* * *

"Do it Now" is a good motto. . . .

* * *

We take off in half an hour. . . .

* * *

It sticks out a mile. . . .

* * *

Isn't it nearly opening time?

* * *

## HE WAS KNACKERED

There was a very uneducated man who by drive, and ruthless methods amassed a large fortune. The older he got, the richer he got, the richer he got the more women he kept, the more women he kept the less use he was to them.

One day he went to the foremost surgeon in the business, and said:

"I want to be castrated."

"You want to be WHAT?"

"I said castrated, my sexual powers are failing."

The surgeon was a bit dubious, but in view of this last statement, and for a consideration of five hundred guineas, he carried out the operation.

A few weeks later the rich illiterate man was in his club, listening to the conversation at the bar, which was "subject normal". "I say Smithers," says one Clubman to his drinking partner, "do you think there's anything in this yarn that if a man gets himself circumcised it improves his sexual performance?"

The rich illiterate retired muttering to himself . . . "*Circumcised*, that was the word I've been trying to think of."

A certain farm labourer was down the bottom meadow when he carelessly cut his thumb in the mowing machine. It bled badly, and they had no first-aid box.

"There's on'y one remedy for that there," said the boss, a sage old farmer – "Ye must goo and put ee in a virgin's bottom, that'll stop the bleeding right away."

The labourer said where would he find such an object, and the farmer replied that a new dairymaid had started that day, he had better go up to the farm house and ask a favour.

The new dairymaid was a good-natured girl, and when Giles explained his difficulty, and showed her his thumb, she without more ado, dropped her bloomers, and bent down.

After a few moments she cried out: "Hey, Garge, that baint my bottom!"

"Baint my thumb, noither."

# WAXING HOT

Some nuns were getting very restless. The weather was very hot, and quarrelling was breaking out.

The Mother Superior called them together and demanded that cards be put on the table – what exactly was the matter.

Nobody would speak until at last a Novice who had not long been in, said: "What this place needs is some healthy males."

The Reverend Mother was shocked, but another, emboldened, said: "Well, she's right, it's only human nature, isn't it?" Mother Superior had met this one before: "Very well then, as it's such hot weather I will issue you all with candles, and you have my dispensation to comfort yourselves with them."

"They're no good, we've tried them," cried several voices.

"Well indeed! when I was young they were all right, what's the objection?"

"Well, Reverend Mother, you get tired of the same thing wick in and wick out!"


# LUCY LOCKET'S POCKET

One morning bright and early an old farmer set off to market to do some shopping and sell two piglets. He and his youngest daughter put the horse in the cart, but Mother decided not to come.

They sold the pigs, bought a few necessities, and set off back. Passing through a lonely wood they were set on by robbers, who took everything, including the farmer's watch. The farmer was broken-hearted, "We're ruined, we're ruined," he kept on saying.

"No Father, we're not," said the girl, "We've still got the pig money, I hid it." "You hid it? But they stripped you!"

"I know, but I stuffed the fivers up my you-know-what."

"Oh, what a pity, what a pity we didn't bring your mother, we'd have saved the sack of flour as well."

## ELASTIC LIMIT

A rather fat bride would wear the latest thing in "foundation garments" and she was indeed strapped in.

The honeymoon was at her mother's house, and her mother was waiting for the floor to start rocking, but nothing much happened. Worried, the old lady crept upstairs and listened at the door. . . .

The trouble had been that the bride's zipper was firmly jammed, and she could not get undressed. Mother arrived just in time to hear:

"It's no use, Darling, we'll never make any progress unless I cut it."

"No no!" shouted mother, "don't be such a fool, just put two fingers in and gradually stretch it!"

## I'LL DO IT TO "SUTURE"!

There was a well-built but rather tom-boyish schoolgirl who was always sliding down the bannisters. One day she lost control, and collided with the knob at the bottom. She was taken to a plastic surgeon, who said of course it would have to be sewn up. He was a kindly old boy, and with a merry twinkle said: "What size shall I make it?"

"Can I have it the same as my mother's?"

"Oh, all right, go back and slide down twice more."

# WARTS AND ALL

The members of the Women's Institute in this particular country parish, fell into a series of quarrels as to whose husband had the biggest phallus.

Feeling ran really high because the Chairwoman said her husband, the Squire, had one so big that there could be no argument, and the matter was not worth discussion.

The women then challenged her to prove this. If her husband would display his weapon, they could judge whether any of their husbands could make a bigger show.

Her Ladyship was now in a right predicament, and she went home and told her husband. He said: "You know I'm small, you've lost your bets." She was so upset that in the end the Squire went to a good friend and said:

"Look here, you've got a huge one. The reputation of the gentry will be tarnished for ever through that damnfool wife of mine, if you won't cooperate."

"What do you want me to do?" said his good friend.

*　　*　　*

The upshot was that it was agreed for the judging to take place in a barn, and the great phallus was to be pushed through a knothole in a screen, so that the owner should not be embarrassed. The Committee of the Institute stood round expectantly, and when the monster was pushed through the knot hole, her Ladyship felt she had won. Alas, one of the women instantly cried:

"Hey, that's the Vicar's, I recognise the wart on the end."

# WITH FUR ROUND IT

A wealthy young man had the chance to take a girl home to her flat. On the way they passed a small furriers shop, and the man said: "If you play ball with me, you can have the best fur coat in that window."

Now the girl was greedy, and she knew a shop where the coats were of a much higher quality. After the rich young man had had his lust on her, she took him round to "Superior Modes", but all he bought her was a rabbit-skin wrap for three pounds.

Home at the weekend she was crying her eyes out, and her father asked her why, so she told him.

"Good God! Didn't your poor mother teach you anything at all about men? Rule number one: When they're hard they're soft: Rule number two: when they're soft they're hard."

# THE LITTLE LESS, HOW MUCH IT IS

A wealthy Bishop had three daughters. He went to his lawyer and said that as their mother was dead he wished to leave a small share of his fortune to two of the girls, but the bulk of it to the third – whichever was the most virtuous.

The lawyer said: "We can't get any further with this my lord, unless you find out definitely which is the most virtuous, you'd better devise a sure test."

The Bishop went away and thought about it, and one summer day he took his oldest daughter, who was twenty, into the shrubbery, and dropped his trousers:

"Forgive me my dear," he said, "but it's only a little test, I want to know if you know what this is?"

"Why, it's a prick," said the girl.

The Bishop thought that wasn't a very good sign of innocence, so he carried out the test with the eighteen-year-old. "It's a prick," she said.

The Bishop hoped things might be a little better with the sixteen-year-old, so he dropped his trousers and said: "My dear, can you tell me what this is?"

"To tell the truth, dear Father, I don't know what to call it."

"Ah my sweet virtuous child, I'm delighted with you, you shall be rewarded. I thought you might say it was a prick."

"My goodness! you don't call that thing a prick, do you?"

## LONGED FOR OLD TIMES

A refugee from Europe had brought his mother to England with him. He prospered, but his widowed mother, who was not really old, began to pine and go into a decline. He decided to send her to a psychiatrist, but to put him in the picture, first. "Don't worry," said the head-shrinker, "I haven't forgotten my Yiddish, I'll be sympathetic."

When the old lady came in he called her "Mudder" and made her feel right at home. Then he held up a spoon, and said: "What's this?"

"Doss iss a leffel." "Fine" (showing fork). "What's this?"

"Doss iss a gappel." "Lovely, what's this?" (holding up a banana).

The widow burst into tears: "Doss iss a phallic symbol."


## SMALL THINGS PLEASE SMALL MINDS

A man was urinating in one of those old-fashioned green iron pee-corners when he heard a lot of giggling, and beheld an eye glued to a crack in the plating.

He was pretty angry, and rushed outside to find a married woman and a girl about fifteen.

"Dammit, you really are vulgar," he shouted, as the girl still giggled.

The mother said: "Oh Sir, take no notice of her, she's only a child, she laughs at any little thing."


## WATERING THE MILK

A little boy had never seen a horse and cart until his family moved to a country town. One day there appeared outside his home a milk float pulled by a horse. He stared in disbelief for some minutes.

When the milkman returned, the little boy said: "You won't get very far!"

"Why not?" enquired the milkman, puzzled.

"All the petrol's just run out and gone down the drain."

## WHO LAVS LAST LAUGHS LAST

There was a fearful row in the nunnery, and in the end the parish priest had to be sent for.

"Sisters, sisters," he said, "what is all this storm about?"

"It's the Reverend Mother," said a bold young nun, "she keeps making the most terrible insinuations about us."

"Indeed," said the priest, "out with it, what's the charge?"

"I haven't charged anybody, and I haven't insinuated anything; I merely demanded to know how it was I found one of the lavatory seats tipped up."

## PIPED

On the Sunday School outing a great deal of lemonade was drunk, and several little girls retired behind a bush to pee, and there was a certain amount of trouble with nettles and thistles.

A small boy who was with them simply pulled out his wee-wee and stood there performing.

"My," said one little girl, "that's a real handy thing to bring on a picnic."

## SONG OF SOLOMON

There was a middle-class suburb of stockbrokers, young businessmen and the like; which was noted for orgies. Wife-swapping was normal, high-class floozies haunted its pubs, while actresses and models kept open house.

The Vicar of the parish, having a rich and generous congregation, was on a good thing. Everybody used to say: "Our Vicar's got a really modern outlook" as they dropped the pound notes on the plate.

However, word got round to the Bishop, who ordered the Vicar to preach strongly against these goings-on. Accordingly, the Vicar got up before the congregation, and said:

"The sins of Sodom are with us, fornication and adultery flourish, and I must, in a fashion warn you, that unless you, as it were, repent, and, so to say, change your ways, you may be, after a manner of speaking, damned."

## HE SAW THE RED LIGHT

The Colonel retired from the Indian army in middle age, and settled in a London flat with his faithful black servant.

After some time he married, and brought his beautiful and toffee-nosed bride home. After the first night he rose at six, as was his custom, to take his constitutional in the park.

The black servant entered the bedroom, pulled all the sheets off the naked bride, and gave her a resounding smack on the backside. . . .

"Dawn him come. Dolly-girl now go back to naughty house."

# BLACK MAGIC

A Missionary came to live with a tribe of Pygmies, and by his gifts of clothing, and superior pills, soon put the Witch Doctor out of business.

However, when the rainy season came the Pygmies developed a peculiar rash behind the knees, and the Missionary failed to cure it. The Pygmies drifted back to the Witch Doctor, who was having great success. The Missionary was beaten, he had to eat humble pie. He went to the Witch Doctor, and said: "Oh father of wisdom, tell me the secret of your cure, and I will reward thee. Blankets? Beads? Mirrors? name thy price and tell me how you get rid of the rash."

The Witch Doctor said that this was most difficult magic, and the only price he was interested in, was a night with the Missionary's daughter in western lingerie, and in the presence of his other wives. The Missionary went home and cried. His daughter (who was as plain as a stick) asked him why, and he told her. Now this girl, ever since she had come to live among these naked savages, had had a craving for black pudding. So, weeping all the while, she said she would reluctantly sacrifice her virginity to save her father's reputation.

Thus the daughter spent a long and busy night in the Witch Doctor's kraal, and returned home late next morning, pale but placid.

Father couldn't wait to hear of her sufferings. . . . "The secret?" he said, "what is this rare medicine, so valuable that only my dear girl's honour could purchase it?"

She yawned, and replied absently, "Oh, that. All he does is cut the tops off their wellingtons."

# BAPTISED BY IMMERSION

Three men went out in a boat to fish in a lake. The protestants were friends – a parson and a minister, but the third, a priest, was a newcomer.

It was a beautiful sunny day, and as they weren't catching much they amused themselves looking at the scenery.

Now it happened that a very shapely young woman came down the strand, stripped off her clothes, and began paddling and bathing in the water. When she saw that she was observed, far from being coy she stood up naked on a rock, exposing her nubile charms, and waved to indicate that she wouldn't mind company.

The men were silent, but after a time the parson said:

"You know, I am a fool, I've left my prayer book on the shore, I hope you will excuse me," with which he upped and walked on top of the water to the shore. He then disappeared into the bushes with the girl, and an hour later he walked back, still dry-shod.

The minister looked thoughtful, then brightened up, and said:

"Dear me, nearly lunch time, and I've left my sandwiches in the car, pray pardon me while I fetch them." With this he stepped out of the boat, walked briskly on the water, and the nude girl was again conducted to a suitable area of green sward.

When the minister at last came back the priest was in a tidy state. He could hardly wait before he leapt overboard, and with no apologies, simply said: "I really must go and get my whisky."

As the priest went down for the third time, and only bubbles came up, the minister turned to the parson and said: "Brother, I know you and I have no time for Popish practices, yet I cannot help feel, before God and the Church, that it would have been an act of Christian charity to have told Father Brown where the stepping-stones were."

## THOSE WHO'RE SAVED

A couple of London whores who had had a very busy season were feeling exhausted, and decided to "Get away from it all". They asked a travel agent, who advised a small town in rural Scotland, where all was peace and quiet.

Off they went, and terrified of being recognised for what they were, dressed very quietly, and behaved in a discreet manner. All was well until the Sabbath, when to keep up the deception, they went off to kirk with the rest of the township.

Now a new minister had arrived, and he was determined that the whole congregation should take part in the hymn singing; this was a fetish of his. It so happened that neither of these whores could sing a note, but to avoid notice, they opened and shut their mouths in time.

But in the middle of the second hymn the minister lost his patience, and shouted in "braid Scots":

"Stop, will ye, stop! It's nae guid enough! There's those that are singin' weel, but there's those who're singin' tae saft."

"Let's get out quick Mary, we're damn-well discovered again."

## MADE IN CAPE HORN?

A man up in Scotland called on a garage where they did a big business in tyres and tyre repairs. Somewhat sheepishly he asked if the Manager would see him in his private office. He then produced from his wallet a somewhat tatty rubber sheath, and said:

"How much wull ye charge tae vulcanise a patch on yon?"

The Manager looked somewhat surprised, but saying nothing examined the article carefully. "About half a crown, and as you can buy a new one for three shillings, I don't see any point in it."

"Verra weel," said the caller, "Ah wull let ye know in a day or so. Ah'll have tae ask them."

"Them, them? Who the hell's them?"

"The Aberdeen Golf Club."

# UN "CONVENT" IONAL!

There was a Catholic priest who had been overworking for years. He finally went to a sympathetic doctor who said: "You're worn out, father, you must go away for a really long holiday." The doctor then wrote to the Bishop, who put up the money for Father Reilly to have three months' paid vacation.

Father Reilly tried everything. He fished, he sailed boats, he walked in the mountains, and soon was again a man in the prime of health.

He had often heard about life in the West End, and as he must soon return to duty, thought he would like to see a strip club. Thus he turned up one night amid the smoke and dim lights, with a double whisky in his hand, enjoying the cabaret. Then the stripper came on, and as she did her act his bulging eyes met hers, and she gave him a wondrous smile.

After her show, the stripper came to the priest's table, placed her bare breasts under his nose, and said: "Can I fetch you another drink, Father Reilly?"

He blenched. "Now by the Holy Church, I'm discovered! I'm utterly ruined! I'll be unfrocked!"

"Don't worry, Father," said the girl, "I'm Sister Theresa, I think we must have the same doctor."

# RAISING COCKS?

On Monday morning teacher asked three boys in the class:

"What was your mother doing when you left the house?"

The first said: "Doing the washing."

The second said: "Vaccing the bedrooms."

The third said: "Getting ready to go out and shoot pheasants."

"What ARE you on about" said teacher.

"Well Miss, me dad's left home and she threw her knickers on the fire and said she was going back to the game."

## TOOK HIMSELF IN HAND

The Jones' were social climbers, and when they moved into a "select" district they decided to ask some of the more superior neighbours in to play bridge one evening. Everything was laid out perfectly, and they packed Junior, who was twelve off to bed, and settled down for a nice evening. Unfortunately, Junior misbehaved. He kept coming back downstairs . . . he couldn't sleep . . . his leg hurt . . . he wanted water. There was interruption after interruption.

Finally a distinguished old gentleman who was a churchwarden and a much respected schoolmaster was appealed to.

"Yes," he said, "I can quieten him, somebody take my hand for ten minutes and leave the rest to me," with which he took Jimmy upstairs.

The rest of the evening was perfect, and not a sound was heard from Junior. As the guests departed, Mrs Jones thanked the old gentleman profusely, and asked him what the secret was.

"Quite easy, Madam, quite easy. I simply taught him to masturbate."


## EXTRA SENSORY PERCEPTION

An old gentleman went into a public convenience and found a grammar school boy about sixteen masturbating himself.

"And what do you think you're doing?" he asked angrily.

"Never mind what I'm doing – duck off," said the boy.

"You think I don't know what you're doing, but I do know what you're doing," went on the old gent.

"You think you know what I'm doing, but you don't," said the boy.

"Well, what are you doing then?" said the man.

"I'm a Christian Scientist, and I'm doing my girl in Edinburgh."

## SHORTCOMING

Two men went behind a hedge to pee. Says one: "I wish I had a big one like my brother's. His is so big he has to hold it with four fingers."

His friend paused, looked, and said:

"But you're holding yours with four fingers!"

"Yes, but I'm wetting on three of them."

## RELIGIOUS PRINCIPLES

There was a young woman who was naturally kind hearted, and she used to go round to her Granny's every Saturday to do the old lady's bedrooms for her. Quite by chance she opened an old box in the wardrobe, and found about five hundred pounds in loose money. She rushed down to Granny, who explained: "It's very simple my dear, next year your Granddad retires, and I've saved and scraped a bit together over the years, so's we can have just a few comforts when we go on pension."

The girl said it was absolutely daft not to put the money into the Post Office to avoid theft, and she kept on about it until Granny agreed to let her take it there and then. It was a fine warm day, so the young woman took a short cut through the woods, to reach the village post office. In the very darkest part, a rough youth jumped out flourishing a knife, and said: "Give me your handbag or I'll cut your throat."

The girl was desperate to distract him. She opened her dress, exposed a very fine pair of bubs, and said: "I'm sure you'd rather play with these."

"No, I must have the money!"

She stepped out of her knickers, lay down on her back, opened her very nice thighs, and said: "Surely a fully blooded male would rather have a virgin than thirty bob out of a handbag?"

He said: "I'd just love to, but I can't."

"Do you mean to say, you snivelling wretch, that you're impotent?"

"No, not at all, but I've given it up for Lent."

## AS IN LIFE SO IN DEATH

Something had gone wrong at the Crematorium. The Manager looked out of his window, and saw a queue of hearses all up the drive. He rushed out and said to his foreman: "What the blazes is the hold up?"

"Sorry boss, but we've got a coffin stuck, it won't go in the oven."

The Manager rushed to have a look, and to his amazement, he saw that it was a Y-shaped coffin. He ran back to the office, rang up the undertaker, and said: "What the hell d'you mean by sending me a Y-shaped coffin?"

"I couldn't help it, I had no choice," said the Undertaker.

"What do you mean – you couldn't help it."

"She was a very sexy young woman."


## THE HEIGHT OF OPTIMISM

Mary: What's the meaning of the saying "The height of optimism?"

Jane: When you're six months gone and rub it with vanishing cream.

\*　　\*　　\*

## CHILD'S ESSAY

Sir Francis Drake circumcised the globe with a forty-foot cutter.

\*　　\*　　\*

## ALL BULL

The Papal Bull is kept at the Vatican to provide milk for the Pope's children.

\*　　\*　　\*

## ASS OVER PIP?

A man came out of a pub, trod on some orange peel, and fell arse over tip. Little girl: Mummy, how did that man know it was a blood orange?

\*　　\*　　\*

## THE FIRST TRADE UNIONIST

Teacher: Who invented the Five Day week?
  Johnny: Please Miss, it was Robinson Crusoe.
  Teacher: What makes you say that?
  Johnny: My Dad says Robinson Crusoe had to work hard all the week and he was always buggered by Friday.

\* \* \*

## DEAD A LONG TIME

Letter from a Coroner to a Town Clerk: I must have a Deputy, I never get a holiday, I haven't slept outside my own bed for twenty years, and my wife badly needs a change.

\* \* \*

## PILLS TO THAT GAME

Mary: What do they call a man whose wife refuses to take the Pill?
  Jane: "Daddy" I should think.

\* \* \*

## WHO'S ZOO

Biology Teacher: How do hedgehogs make love?
  Bright Student: With the utmost caution, I suspect!

\* \* \*

# LIMERICKS III

There was a young laundress named Gert
Who couldn't get into her skirt,
Her dildo she'd smothered
With starch which had covered
The front of a clergyman's shirt.

A reckless young sculler named Box
Forced the Oxford crew on to the rocks,
The Eight shouted: "Rowlocks!
You've ripped off our bowlocks
And terribly injured our cox."

There was a young lady named Lee
Whose quim was as small as could be
When needing a lay
A search fee she'd pay
And loan the binoculars, free.

A pious young widow named Dove
Was wearing black garters, for love,
"They remind me," she'd say,
As she stripped for a lay
"Of many who've gone up above."

A sexy young lady named Hall
Whose tits were exceedingly small
Made up for the lack
With a very large crack,
Her love life was "having a ball".

# The Crusader and the Chastity Belt

There was a Baron who had a most beautiful young wife, and he wished to ride forth on the Crusades. Knowing his wife's passionate nature, and that he would be gone at least a year, he consulted his Magician, who advised fitting the lady with a chastity belt. So the Baron went to the best man in the business, and duly the lady, although protesting a great deal, was locked up in it.

"But my Lord," she cried: "If by any mischance you are killed, I shall be encased in it to my grave." Her husband took the point, and consulted with his Magician again, following which, he announced to all the Court that he would leave the key with the most trustworthy man in England, namely, the Archbishop of Canterbury.

\* \* \*

Thus it came to pass a few days later, a ship loaded with Crusaders was just casting off from Dover when a very dusty Archbishop arrived on the quayside on a very exhausted horse. . . .

"Hey!" he shouted, "this is the wrong key!"

"You're telling me!" said the Baron.

## THE BITER BIT

There was a King who wanted to go on the Crusades, but he was very worried about his wife, who was a bit too oo-lalla to be left alone for a long time. The King consulted his Bishop, who had a bright idea. He explained that he knew a smith so cunning that he could make a suitable device to fix on the lady and keep the men off.

Thus it came to pass that the Bishop produced a man-trap device with fearful teeth, so set that if any male approached it, it would snap shut, with devastating results.

When the King returned from his travels he lined all the Courtiers up, and demanded from each in turn, whether he had behaved like a true gentleman to the King's wife. Each swore that he had, and the King noted with grim satisfaction that each had a high-pitched voice. Only the Court Jester acted awkward, he wouldn't answer any questions at all.

"He seems to have lost his tongue!" said the King.

"Indeed he has," said the Bishop.


## DIRTY DOG FASHION

There was a miner who went off to the pit for the afternoon shift, but when he got there it was to find that there was a breakdown in the plant, and they were all sent home again.

The miner returned to find his plump wife bending down over the sink, washing up. Without a word he upped her skirts, dragged her drawers down and quickly had his will on her.

Having finished he gave her bare behind two or three vicious blows.

"You nasty rotten bleeder!" she said, "I stood there and let you have your will on me, and all the thanks I got for it was a good 'idin'."

"That was for not looking round to see who it was," he said.

# WAAL BRUSH MA NUTS!

There was an American gentleman of the Deep South who was proud of his family and traditions. One day there called a distant cousin, an Englishman. A splendid meal was laid on, followed by genuine old Scotch, and ceegars worth five dollars apiece. Just "Southern hospitality".

"Now, Sir," said the host, "As Ah wuz naat a-ware of yo' arrival, Ah arranged to go to Rotary right now, but my wife, wa-al, I guess she'll entertain ya, an' show y' th' garden an' ma prerry lawns." With which he departed.

The wife showed the guest the house and garden, and then, in a shady corner of the lawn, began to undress. "I say!" said the Englishman, "I'm not an utter cad you know."

She explained that this was just part of famous "Southern hospitality" – what else did her husband mean by "show him the lawns"? They couldn't do it in the house with the children in bed, now, could they?

She lay on her back, the Englishman stripped and got on with it. Quite soon the husband returned however, but the first the guest knew about it was when he heard the husband's voice from the porch of the house:

"Sadie, Sadie, aint y'shure ashamed! Is this what you call Southern hospitality. Arch up you' back at once, an' raise the ge'man's boils off of the demp grass!"

## SPIRITUAL NEEDS

There was an Irishman hastening up and down a train, putting his head in every compartment and asking for a priest. He was clearly distressed, and when he came back a second time, a Methodist Minister looked up from the Church Herald and said: "We are all brothers in the Lord, although I am only a humble Methodist minister, if you will take me to your friend who is ill or distressed, I will comfort him as well as I may."

"It's meself that's after bein' distressed!" said the Irishman, "and noone else besides."

"What can I do for you brother?"

"Nothing! I must have a priest, I'm stuck for a bottle opener."

## COFFEE IN BED

There was a soldier who had been abroad for some years, and his turn came round for home leave. He gave his wife the date, but by getting a lucky air-lift he arrived a week early. His wife, who had had a black baby in his absence, was startled to see the husband coming up the garden path, and she hastily hid the baby in the wardrobe.

Husband came in, brown from the African sun, ordered his wife upstairs immediately, and followed her. While she was undressing he casually looked in the wardrobe, and saw the coloured child.... .

"I – I'm sorry about that," stammered the wife.

"So am I," said the husband, "how did the little devil manage to follow me all this way?"

## COULDN'T LOVE FOR TOFFEE

A married couple began to have rows, and the upshot of it was she locked him out of her bedroom for three weeks. He slept in the spare room, and seemed so little bothered that she greatly regretted her rashness.

One night she was just retiring when there came a knocking on the door.

"It's me knocking," he said.

"Of course I know it's you knocking."

"But I bet you don't know what I'm knocking with, or you'd open the door."

"Will you let me have it darling, if I let you in?"

"Of course I will, it's here, ready in my hand, I'm dying to give it you."

She threw her nightie off and slid back the bolts.

He entered and gave her a tin of caramels.

## HOLEY SMOKE?

Two Irishmen were approached by the priest, and asked what they would give up for Lent.

After discussion Kelly said he would pack in smoking. Reilly said he would renounce sex.

Two weeks later Reilly was asleep and having a marvellous dream in which he lay in a bath full of beer watching a TV horserace in which his 20–1 fancy was leading the field. . . . His wife shook him awake.

"Pat," she said, "Pat wake up, I want to tell yez something."

"What is it now woman?" said her husband irritably.

"Pat, today I saw Mike Kelly smoking back o' the bike shed."

# HOPE FOR THE FUTURE GENERATION

An earnest spinster schoolteacher got herself seduced by a preacher.

As she rose from her bed and began to get dressed, she said: "Oh, I can't get up in front of those children next week and tell them to be good, now I'm nothing but a regular sinner!"

"Regular sinner, Gwendoline, you've only done it once!"

"Yes, but we've got the whole weekend in front of us haven't we?"

# HACKING

There was an English working man who won some money on the "pools" and decided that he and his wife should "see the world". However, by the time they got as far as Texas they had spent much more than they bargained for.

There was a rodeo advertised, with many cash prizes on offer, so in they went. The star event was for a "greenhorn" to ride the bucking broncho.

Over the loudspeakers came the message, that if any amateur could stay on the unbroken bronc for fifteen seconds he should have a thousand dollars. Many brave young men had a go, but they all got hurt, for he was indeed a vicious animal.

Suddenly, Dad got up and said he'd have a go. Mother clutched his jacket, but he slipped out of it, and entered the ring. Everybody laughed, but he stayed on, and collected the thousand dollars.

When he got back to his seat, his wife said: "But you've never been on a horse in your life, how DID you do it?"

"I know Mother, but don't you recall how when we went on honeymoon you had the whooping cough?"

# DOING IT THE HARD WAY

There was a man whose wife led him a hell of a life. He went to consult an old friend on his problems, and the friend says: "Do you ever have sex with her?"

"What! That skinny old stringbag, why it would kill her."

"There you are then," said the friend, "get on a diet of oysters and raw egg, get in training, then do her three times every night. She can't refuse you, that's grounds for a divorce, but at the end of a month she'll be dead."

The man went into training, and did as he was bid. Three weeks later his old friend met him in the street. His back was bowed, his hands trembled, his head shook, his eyes rolled about, and he could scarcely walk.

"Ha," said his friend, "how's your wife?"

"Well, Jack, outwardly she looks very plump and well, but I'm laughing, because, although she doesn't know it, she's only got a week to live!"

# STORY WITH NO WHISKERS ON IT

A businessman had a shapely young wife and he rather neglected her in favour of the Stock Exchange. When she suggested a holiday he said: "You go off my dear, I've got a lot to do at the office."

She fixed herself up for a fortnight away, and the husband was very pleased, until he found out it was at a Nudist Camp, when he began to be very suspicious. In the end, when she swore to be modest in her conduct, he let her go.

When the wife came home and went to bed with her husband, she tried to get undressed in the dark, which was unusual. He switched the light on again, and observed that she was bare at the fork, her dark brown curly thatch was missing.

His worst fears were aroused. He demanded an instant explanation: "And it had better be good, or you're divorced, and without a penny!"

The girl said it was that long spell of wet weather.

"Wet weather?"

"Yes, it rained three days running, there was nothing to do but sit in the Social Hut and play cards."

"And now you're going to say you lost your Ace of Spades – come on, the truth girl, the truth?"

"I'm telling you, we played Strip Poker."

"How could you play Strip Poker in a Nudist Camp?"

"We used pairs of tweezers. Oh darling, I had a most terrible bad run of cards, and you wouldn't want your little wife to come home without any eyebrows now, would you?"

## PUSHING THE BOAT OUT

An innocent girl got a date with a man and they went for a long walk in the country. Coming to a pond, the young man boldly flashed himself out and urinated into the water.

The girl was in need too, and thought if he could make a splash, she could, so she dropped her drawers and did the same.

"Oh dear," she said, "I think I wee-weed into a canoe!"

"No dear, that was just your own reflection."

## SOLD HIM THE DUMMY

An ignorant man was left some money in a will, provided he had an heir. As he had been married several years with no offspring, he consulted the doctor. The doctor said, after tests, that this man could never become a father. "Doctor, I could afford to pay you a hundred pounds if you could solve this one for me." "Easy," said the doctor, "have you never heard of A.I.D.?"

The man said he hadn't. The doctor explained that the woman was made pregnant by another man's seed. The patient said that under no circumstances would he have another man doing his wife.

"Don't be silly, there's no intercourse involved, leave this to me." He went on to say that the wife must come to his surgery next evening, to see if she approved of the Donor. A suspicious husband followed behind. He peeped through the curtains, he saw his wife introduced to a handsome young man, he saw the doctor called to the telephone, and he saw the doctor leave to answer an urgent call.

When he resumed his vigil at the window he saw his naked wife thrashing about under the Donor, who was giving her the belting of a lifetime. When the doctor returned up the garden path he was met by the husband, who said:

"Come and look doctor"—the doctor peeped—"you know doctor, you said there would be no intercourse, and it's a good job I trust you, or else I would have swore he was doing her."

## SEDUCTION NO RAPE

There was a convent bred girl who went out with a man who used to kiss her goodnight against a dark wall. She began to get slightly worried, and she went back to the convent to ask for advice.

"Tell me all about it from the beginning my child," said the Mother Superior. The girl explained that at first this young man got out a hard thing and pressed it against her. After a few weeks he was pushing an inch, and then two inches up her wee-wee. Lately it had been five inches, and last night it was six.

"And what is it you want to ask me, my child?"

"Well, Reverend Mother, I want to know if I'm taking too much risk, I mean, do you think that if I let him go on like this, one night he might rape me?"

## CAVES OF DELIGHT

A widow married for the second time, and she was greatly disappointed with her new husband's equipment. One evening she was in such a bad temper he asked what was the matter.

"I had a bad dream last night."

"Tell me about it?"

"I dreamed I was at a big auction sale, and men were bidding for phalluses. The long ones made up to five pounds, the thick ones were fetching six pounds, and the long thick ones over ten pounds."

"I see, and what about those like mine?"

"Those like yours were withdrawn, not reaching the reserve."

The husband said that was a strange coincidence, for he too had had a similar dream. . . .

"I dreamed they were auctioning quims, the tight muscular ones fetched really high bids, and the unbroken ones over twenty quid each."

"And now I suppose you are going to make out that one like mine was considered useless?"

"Not at all dear, that's where they held the auction."

# HE BELTED HER WELL

A young bride was very ill-educated. When she found herself pregnant she rushed off to the doctor for advice. He told her a number of things. Then she asked: "What is the best position for actually having the baby?"

The doctor said the nurse would see to all that. The young woman explained that her husband was just taking her out to Arabia where he'd got a good job, there would only be native help: "What's the best English position for delivering it?"

"Exactly the same as when you conceived it."

"Great heavens doctor, do you mean I've got to give birth in the back of a car parked in a field with my ankles lashed up in the safety belts?"


# SINGULAR

A young woman went to the doctor and said she wanted an operation or some drugs or something, as, try as she might, she could not conceive a baby, and her husband was nearly worn out.

"How long have you been married my dear?"

"Two years doctor."

"Two years! Good lord, give Nature a chance girl, go away and keep trying. If in another four years, nothing has happened, come back and we will see if intervention is indicated."

The woman said: "But doctor, I was brought up in total innocence, ignorance would be a better word, but the one thing I've known since I was at school, was this, that if you wanted a baby, all you had to do was have one night in bed with a man."

"Ah yes," said the old doctor, *"but only when you're single."*

# CHALKING IT UP

A man lived an average sort of life, and he died, and went up to meet Saint Peter, and said: "Can I come into Heaven?"

"Heaven," said Peter, "this isn't Heaven." He went on to explain that the Pearly Gates were much higher up, and could only be reached by very long ladders, which varied according to circumstances. . . .

"You take this chalk and start climbing. For each sin of adultery, fornication, lechery, or whatever, you chalk off one rung."

The man kept going for ages, his legs ached, his arms ached, and he met no one. All at once he saw a fellow in a curious garb descending the neighbouring ladder.

"Excuse me, Sir," he said, "are you by any chance an angel going back for more candidates?"

"No indeed, I'm the Archbishop of Canterbury going back for more chalk."

# A LOAD OF TRIP-LETS

There was a young parson whose wife was expecting, and he was pacing up and down outside a Maternity Ward.

At last the midwife came out and said: "Congratulations, you've got a bonny pair of twins!"

"Oh dear, oh dear," said the parson, "I'm afraid that's the end of our marriage, I never thought she would be unfaithful."

"Unfaithful, don't talk daft."

"But you see nurse, I was only wicked once, the other one isn't mine."

## WHIRLED AROUND

There was a man in a strange town, and he thought he might as well go to a dance. He entered the local "Palais", but before long he was taken short, and not knowing the place, he could not find the toilets. He asked an attendant, who replied in an unfamiliar dialect that it was: "Up thur, and rahnd thur, and up them stairs."

More and more desperate he wandered through store rooms and attics, and in the end did the job in a cleaners' cupboard (as he thought).

When the young man got back down to the big ballroom, the place was empty, except for the commissionaire.

"Where have they all gone?"

"Where have they all gone? They've all gone to look for the rotten bleeder that used the fan room as a lavatory."

## GROUP SEX

A young woman rushed into a police station, and said: "I've been graped!"

"Beg pardon, Miss, do you mean you've been raped?"

"No Sergeant, there was a bunch of them."

# THE LONG AND THE SHORT OF IT

There was a strongminded woman married to a meek little man, though all his pals at work kept telling him to assert himself.

One day she told him: "We're going up town this afternoon to buy you a new pair of trousers." Off they went to the shop, and she chose the trousers for him. The shop assistant said: "Now these come in several styles, do you want button flies or zipper flies?"

"Zipper," replied the man, quickly.

"Very good, Sir, and do you want a five-inch zip or a ten-inch?"

"Ten inch," said the man, before his wife could intervene.

\* \* \*

When they got outside, she was furious. "You!" she said, "You and your ten-inch zip! Why you remind me of the man who lives next door to my father. Every morning he goes down his garden and unlocks his garage, then he opens the eight-foot double doors, then he wheels his bike out."

## TOOK HIS GIRL FOR A SPIN

There was a girl went home and told her mother she must break her engagement. Her mother asked why, and she said: "He's too tall, and too fond of practical jokes." Mother explained that tall men were to be preferred, and a sense of humour was vital in marriage. . . . "Tell me more about the trouble – confide frankly in your mother," she said.

"Well, Mother, when he says goodnight to me in the back porch he puts his hand in my blouse." "That's no harm," says mother, "go on."

"Then he lifts my skirt, pulls down my knickers, and puts it in."

"After all," said mother, "this is the age we live in, and you ARE engaged."

"But Mother, next he straightens his legs, lifts me clear of the ground, and applies his famous sense of humour."

"A little uncomfortable perhaps," said mother, "but hardly grounds for a broken engagement."

"Ho, alright Mother! How would YOU like to be spun round like an aeroplane propellor?"

## STRIPPING THE OLD GEYSER

*Workmen's Time Sheets received by Borough Surveyor*
4 hours stripping old geyser in bathroom (would not get hot).

\*    \*    \*

Trimming the virgins on either side of the highway, 8 hours.

\*    \*    \*

4 hours mating on sewers.

\*    \*    \*

8 hours mating with tractor (horse not available).

\*    \*    \*

Half day, stripping young Ivy at rear of Park Pavilion.

\*    \*    \*

# HE MUST HAVE BEEN A LITTLE WET

There was a woman with a large family of small children. As she was married to a jockey they were quite well off, and set on an Au Pair girl. The first evening the Au Pair arrived the woman was called away to a sick relative. She said to her: "I want you to bath all the children, littlest first, and put them to bed. I warn you, some of the boys are little devils."

"I am peasant daughter, ver' sthrong, und I hab brudders, I vill conquer, Madame, you vill see."

So the woman went out, and when she came back she asked how the bathing time had gone. The girl explained that with only one exception she had washed and bedded the kids with no trouble. . . .

"Only dat big boy mit der red 'air, 'e stroggle und fight sometink terrible. I am mit der blows smitten, but I overcomen him at last."

"With red hair?" said the mother, "my God, that was my husband!"

Here lieth an innocent maid
By a medical student betrayed
Caesarian section
Came after injection,
She thought he was teaching First Aid.

A lesbian just out of jail
Was asked how she managed for tail
Said: "Up inside 'holloway'
Putting dildol away,
A Miss is as good as a Male."

There was a young baker named Hall
Whose wife had a child every Fall,
His partner, an oaf
Said: "I use my loaf
My Missus has no kids at all."

A jungle explorer named Bunce
Took photos of native-girls' fronts
In no beads enveloped,
But they're not developed,
He's going again in twelve months.

There was a young sailor named Viner
Who failed to get in a vagina
When visualised frontal
It ran horizontal
He forgot he was stationed in China.

# Cock and Bull Story

A farmer kept the parish bull, and made a good thing out of the stud fees. However, during a busy harvest season he and his older son had to be down in the fields a great deal.

The farmer said to his young son, who was twelve, "Sam, stay in the yard, if anybody brings a cow, turn the bull out, and take three pounds off them."

The boy had several customers, then things went quiet, and he was just about to lock the bull up when a big angry-looking man came up carrying a shotgun and a whip.

"I'm farmer Giles," he said, "where's your father?"

"He's out, Sir, and my brother's out. There's only me in, can I help you?"

"No you can't, your brother has put my daughter in the family way!"

"That's right, Sir, you'll have to see father, I don't know how much he charges for Harry."


## LOOKING FOR A WIRE

There was a young working man whose wife was expecting their first baby. Mother-in-law, who was as thrilled as the rest of them, lived a long way off. Mother-in-law insisted that she should be sent a telegram immediately the child arrived, giving full details. Son-in-law said he was much too shy to write such things out in front of a Post Office girl.

After a deal of argument, Mother-in-law said it would do if the telegram was in code.

The great day arrived, and Mother-in-law was somewhat surprised to receive a telegram reading: BICYCLE ARRIVED SAFELY PUNCTURED BACK AND FRONT PUMP AND TOOLBAG MISSING.

## SHE'D HAD A NIBBLE

There was a small boy who kept biting his nails. His mother warned him that if he didn't stop he'd get like *that* (pointing to a pregnant woman sitting opposite in the bus).

From then on, the boy never took his gaze off the woman's belly, until in the end she angrily said: "Little boy why are you staring at me?"

Down the crowded bus rang his reply: "Because I know how you got like that."

## CIRCUMSTANTIAL EVIDENCE

There was a commercial traveller called on a farmer to sell him a new tractor. The farmer didn't want a new tractor. "In fact, I'm thinking of packing in farming," he said.

The traveller was persistent. The farmer was obdurate.

Finally the farmer said: "Look here, I'm in real trouble, and if you can get me out of it, I'll buy a tractor." He went on to explain his problem. The previous afternoon he had brought home a new cow. . . .

"When I went to milk her she turned out a devil. She brought round her right leg and kicked the bucket over, so I tied her leg to the stall. Then she brought round her left leg, and kicked ME, so I lashed it to the other post. Next she swung her tail and knocked my hat off, so I tied her tail to the rafters.

"By this time I was sweating, so I took my coat off. Then I needed a piss, so I undid my trousers and stood behind the cow to relieve myself.

"At that moment my wife walked in, and if you can convince HER. . . ."

## GETTING DOWN TO IT

There was a widow who had one son, and when he got married she was envious. Her son and his wife had the front parlour, and every evening she used to go and listen outside the door.

Every evening after tea she would hear her son say: "Come on Mary, let's have half an hour on the rug." Sometimes it would be the girl who would say: "Don't bother about the telly Jack, let's have a bit of time on the rug together."

Mother's suspicions got worse when she once heard:

"Whatever else happens, Mother mustn't find out about this."

Christmas came, and imagine mother's surprise when the couple presented her with a lovely rug, assuring her they had made it themselves!

## PRAYING FOR IT

A woman was being treated by a doctor for sore knees. She made no improvement so he said: "Look, something's rubbing the skin off your knees as fast as it heals – is it prayer?"

"No Doctor, it's my husband, he will have his sex dog-fashion on the floor, and in no other way."

The doctor sent for the man, and gave him a telling-off: "There's plenty of other positions for sex," he told him.

"No Doctor, no there aint, not if we're going to watch the telly as well."

## HAND REARED

A man went to his doctor because he was so run down.

"Do you get a regular sex life?" asked the doctor.

"Oh yes," said the man, "with my wife, twice a day."

"I see, anyone else?"

"Yes, Doctor, with my secretary, twice a day."

"Now you look here young man, you'll have to take yourself in hand."

"But I do Doctor, twice a day."

# THE PEDLAR CALLED

A busy Registrar of Births Deaths and Marriages noticed that on four birth notifications for the same day, the father was the same Joe Bloggs, though the mothers lived far apart.

He made it his business to visit the father on pretext of checking the facts: he turned out to be a little runt of a middle-aged plumber.

"Look here," said the Registrar, "North Side, South Park, East End, and Western Boulevard, all miles apart. And four in one day, how DO you manage it?"

"It's quite easy, Sir, you see, I've got a bicycle."


# THE PEEHOLE

There was a most virtuous spinster, who boasted that no man had ever been near her. When she was forty-five a wide boy married her for her considerable fortune. When he went along to draw a couple of thousand to put on the gee-gees, her solicitor said:

"She tells me the marriage is not consummated, therefore it's not a marriage. If you don't give her what she got married for, not only do you draw nothing, but she can divorce you, and make you pay the costs."

"But listen mister, I can't, I can't, her quim's too small!"

"What do you mean, too small? You ought to be damn pleased."

"I tell you it's too small ever to operate."

The solicitor sent for a doctor neighbour of his to come over and hear the tale.

"What do you MEAN by small?" said the latter. "Is it like a banana split?"

"Smaller than that."

"Is it like the cleft of my chin?" – "Smaller than that!"

"Like a cowrie shell?" – "No."

"Well, for cripes sake, what is it like?"

"Listen, Doctor, have you ever seen a mouse's earhole?"

## LOVE'S ENTANGLEMENT

There was a rich old devil who married a young shapely piece, and really fancied himself in bed.

On the first night he began to grind away, and soon she was squeaking and squawking. "Am I stretching you honey?" he chortled through his toothless gums.

"No dammit, but your truss is tangled with my whiskers."


## PUTTING UP THE MAINMAST

There was a low-class whore who swore she could take any man. A Portsmouth sailor took her round the back of a pub and put her against the wall. She began to get really frightened: "Here," she said, "steady up past my heart."

"Never mind your heart, hold your hat on."


## UPS AND DOWNS OF MARRIAGE

A man went home and told his wife he had received a great honour – he had been asked to lecture to the Rotary Club.

"What will you lecture on dear?"

"Flying," he said.

"Why you silly fool, you've had no experience of flying since you left the Royal Flying Corps in 1918, and then you got grounded!"

They had quite an argument, and the man knew his wife was right, but he wasn't going to admit it. Privately he decided to lecture on sex instead, but he didn't tell her.

\* \* \*

A day or two later the wife met another Rotary wife. "Did you hear how my husband's talk went?" she enquired.

"Yes, they said it was very good indeed."

"Was it, you amaze me!"

"Why do you say that, dear?"

"Well, my husband has only been up three times in his life; the first time he was sick, the second time, he blacked out, and the third time, his hat blew off."

## HIGH OCTANE

A man had the bonnet of his car up, and his head inside.

A drunk came by, and became a nuisance. . . .

"Wash marrer ol' man, gorrer sphot o' trouble. What ish it, eh?"

The motorist was abrupt. . . . "Piston broke."

"Ah, thash bad luck, pishton broke, sho am I, sho am I."

## WRONG ORGAN

There was a girl sitting on the settee in the front room with her new young man. After speaking about the weather he fell into a long silence.

"Look here," she said, "when you have a girl all by herself, can't you do something?"

"Oh, ar," he said, with which he produced a mouthorgan and began to play it.

## VERY INDUSTRIOUS

The famous Climax engines and fork-lift trucks are made in Coventry. A group of students from the University of Warwick were given a "project" namely, to research into the habits of young married couples who both went to work, to see if it affected their sex life. They went from door to door with their questionnaires, and one student was greeted by a smashing young housewife, who said, Yes, she was willing to give information.

"How old are you?"

"I'm 22, he's 25."

"I see, and how often do you have sex?"

"Every night, and twice on Saturdays and Sundays."

"Now, Madam, this is rather personal, and if you feel you do not want to answer it, it's up to you, but, er, how long does it generally take you to get to orgasm?"

"I beg your pardon, I don't follow?"

"How long does it take you to reach the climax?"

"Well, ten minutes if I catch the bus, but half an hour if I have to walk."

# RATTLING IDEA

Some Secondary School girls were having an intimate conversation about what they did when they went out with boyfriends.

"I always carry a sheath in my handbag," said the first.

"I get some pills off my mother's dressing table," said the next.

There was silence. "Come on, Theresa, what do you do?"

"You know Catholics aren't allowed to use those things, they're artificial."

"Yes, but you're not frustrated, what do you DO?"

"I carry a biscuit tin with a few stones in it."

(Both together): "A biscuit tin! How does that work?"

"Easy, I make him stand on it, and when it starts to rattle I kick it from under him."

# DUCKING THE ISSUE

Three girls in distress went to a centre of Religious Healing. The Reverend Master in charge asked what could he do for them? One had got tiny breasts and wanted them bigger, one had got legs like beansticks and she wanted plump sexy thighs, the third was doubled up in a wheelchair.

It was explained to them that this was much too tall an order for a provincial healing centre, but if they were to go to the River Jordan and totally immerse themselves, they would stand a good chance, provided they had *faith* as well. The Reverend Master, who had questioned them closely, was satisfied that Mary and Jean had faith, but about Agnes in the wheelchair he was very doubtful. However she swore she had faith too, and he sent them off to the Jordan with the necessary documents and introductions.

When the great day arrived, Mary went first, totally immersed herself in the icy stream, and came out with a superb pair of breasts.

Jean went next, bravely ducked, and walked up with splendid thighs and a round bottom to match.

It was necessary to get local assistance to get the wheelchair out, and when it was pulled up the bank the anxious watchers noticed that it now had a brand new pair of tyres.

# IT DEPENDS WHAT YOU MEAN

A young married man was thrilled when his wife was expecting their first child. As soon as she was in labour he took her off to the Maternity Hospital.

The same night he rushed up to the hospital enquiry desk to enquire.

"Ward 3B," they said, "and she's had triplets."

He ran up the stairs and was barging into the ward when a frosty Sister promptly threw him out again.

"How dare you come in here, you're not sterile!" she said.

"Sterile! Me? I should bloody well think I'm not sterile, I've just fathered triplets!"


# ACTIONS SPEAK LOUDER THAN WORDS

There was a Professor of English in the University of Oxford, who was a very great stickler for the correct use of words. Unfortunately he had a termagant wife who led him a hell of a life.

One day this nagging bitch announced that she would go and have a holiday with her mother. She packed her bags, summoned a taxi, and departed.

The Professor couldn't wait. He took the very sexy housemaid into his study, pressed a five pound note into her hand, and found her only too willing.

Unfortunately the wife had forgotten her handbag, and ten minutes after departure, she returned. Finding no one downstairs, and hearing some unusual noises she rushed aloft and opened the study door. The maid's knickers and bra were on a chair, and the maid was not inside them. The Professor was far too busy to notice her entry until she shouted:

"John, John, I AM surprised!"

Occupied as he was, yet this gross abuse of English pulled him up short:

"No no, my dear, it is WE who are surprised, YOU are amazed."

# THE BLACK PUDDING CLUB?

There was an old Professor of Anthropology at Oxford who had a hatred of women, and especially of women students. One day he noticed half a dozen of them sitting in the front row, legs and busts in full view.

The Professor addressed the class: "Gentlemen, this morning we are going to talk about the Trobriand Islanders. This race of naked barbarous savages never wash, and they smell. They live upon herbs which give their breath a foul odour. Their male members are twice normal size, and they place on a ring of thorns before intercourse. In these wretched islands there are four men to every woman, so even the ladies of Lady Margaret Hall might find a husband there."

The girls were so disgusted they rose in a body and walked out.

As they got to the door he shouted: "Don't hurry, the steamers only go every six months."

## APPRECIATIVE AUDIENCE

There was a young married woman who went to her doctor for some help. She explained that her husband never made love to her, was she lacking in something, she was certainly frustrated. The doctor examined her all over, one excuse was as good as another, for she had a really shapely body.

"It's not you, it's him," he said, "but put one of these pills in his tea at breakfast time, and I think by bedtime he'll be a bit randy." He added: "Come back and let me know, because they're experimental."

Two days later the woman was back, and she was furious.

"Didn't it work then?"

"Work! Work! We were just sitting down to tea when he glared at me with lust in his eyes. Then he swept all the crocks on the floor, dragged the cloth off, dragged my knickers off, and did me violently straight across the table. I was never so angry in my life."

"Angry, madam? I thought that was just what you wanted."

"I said angry, Doctor. Why, I shall never dare go in that branch of Lyons again."

## BUCKED UP

There was a man whose wife was frigid and a shrew. He had a rotten life with her. Yet, when he died she gave him a posh funeral, and even went to the Spiritualists to see how he was getting on.

The Spiritualist said that for a suitable fee he thought he could get in touch with the dear departed, and after a little effort, with the widow and her relations sitting in the dark round a table, a signal came through.

"Hush," hissed the Spiritualist, "I am in tune with our Brother, speak to him Mrs Faggott."

"Hallo Harry, are you very happy dear?"

"Yes my dear, I am more happy than words can speak."

"Oh, I'm glad of that Harry, what's it like being an angel in heaven?"

"Angel in heaven! I'm a buck rabbit on Salisbury Plain!"

# CAUGHT IN A NET

A woman went to a solicitor and said she must have a divorce.

Was her husband unfaithful? – No, nothing like that, she wanted a divorce for "cruelty".

She went on to explain that her husband was peculiar, he had a twisted mind. He never played billiards but with crooked cues, he liked to shave standing on his head . . . whatever he did, he did the hard way.

The solicitor said this was eccentricity but not cruelty, it was not enough. "But," said the wife, "he wants to make love in the garden."

"Good lord woman!" said the solicitor, losing patience, "that's a compliment. . . ."

"All right," said the woman, "then YOU try having intercourse standing up in a hammock."

# DARKER SIDE OF LOVE

*The following are actual reports from a Northern Matrimonial Court:*

(a) Young woman: My husband's a sexual monster, I must leave him.

Magistrate: What do you mean "sexual monster"?

Y.W.: He wants it nearly every night!

M.: Of course he does, that's what he married you for.

Y.W.: But he wants it in a most unnatural way!

M.: Aha, that's different. Tell us about his bestial practices.

Y.W.: Well, he wants it with the light on!

(b) Wife: I demand a divorce, I can't stay with him.

Magistrate: On what grounds, Madam?

Wife: Unreasonable demands! He's wrecking my health with his lusts.

Mag.: I see, well what "unreasonable demands" – how often?

Wife: I can't bear to talk about it, it's disgusting!

Mag.: Come, Madam, we can't help you if you won't help us. How often?

Wife: Twice a week!

Mag.: Good God almighty! Women have stood where you're standing now, and called twice a week desertion!

Enoch and Eli had been going to see Wolverhampton Wanderers for years. Every home game they would meet behind the Molineux end goal, and cheer their team. Then, one season early, Enoch failed to turn up. Three times he missed. Eli sought him out:

"I ay seen yo down the Wanderers lately, where've y'been?"

Enoch explained that he had married a plump and passionate wife. Every time he was getting ready to go to the match, she would grab him and pull him down on to the hearthrug. . . .

Eli explained that it was quite unmanly to be ruled by a woman in this manner: "Next Satday, if her does that, yo must pull her bloomers down and put her acrost yer knee, and slap her backside good and hard. If her cries, do it harder, then come to the match."

Enoch swore that he would, but he didn't turn up at the game.

Eli was furious, and quickly sought his mate for an explanation.

"Did y'do what I told yer?"

"Ar, well, I caught hold of her and put her over me knee. I dragged her drawers down, I raised me 'ond, but well, the Wolves haven't been playing very well lately, have they?"

# A WILLING STAND-IN

Two working men were leaning on a bar discussing marriage.

"My wife's cold, dead cold," complained one, "I'm only too anxious any time, but she always says she don't feel like it."

"Ah that's it," said the other, "you lack technique."

"What the hell's that when it's out?"

"Now listen, you nit. When you go home Friday, give her a box of chocolates. After tea, fetch a bottle of her favourite tipple. Then take her on your knee, open her dress and play with her tits for an hour. . . ."

"Yes," said the husband, "then what?"

"Take her pants off, lay her on her back, stroke her thighs, play with her clit. . . ."

"Then what?"

"Send for me."

# MORE HOLEY THAN THOU

There was a small boy who was always a chatterbox.

One morning, after Daddy had gone to work, he said:

"Mamma, you know you went out to Grannie's all day yesterday."

"Yes, my son. What about it?"

"Well, Daddy came home after lunch, and do you know what him and the maid were doing in your bedroom. . . ."

"Be quiet! How dare you talk like that!" she said. Then, after a moments reflection: "Jimmy, when Mamma wants you to speak about it she will ask you."

That same evening, when Daddy came home for his evening meal, and they were all seated at the table, Mother said: "Now Jimmy, what was it you were telling me this morning about Daddy and the maid yesterday?"

"Well, Mamma, I was playing at hiding in the wardrobe when Daddy brought Mary in, and I peeped out and they were taking their clothes off. . . ."

"Really, my dear," said Father, "this is most unfair. . . ."

"You shut up!" said Mother, "I'm off to my solicitor in the morning; go on Jimmy, there's a good boy."

"Well she lay on the bed, and he got on top of her."

"Yes, go on."

"Then they started to do what you and Uncle John did last summer when Daddy was away on his business trip."

# GREEK COMEDY

A labourer who lived in a very small cottage went to the Marriage Guidance Council and said that his sex life was unsatisfactory, his wife said she didn't enjoy it.

He was instructed that variation might make it more interesting. For instance, why not try the Greek position? He went away, thoughtful.

Three months later he was back, still in trouble. . . .

"Did you try the Greek position?" – "Yes."

"And your wife didn't like it?" "No guvnor, she loved it."

"Then why are you back here?" – "We had to give it up."

"Why, for goodness' sake?" "Well guv, doing it like that, the kids kept laughing at us."

# LIMERICKS V

A land-hungry farmer named Jakers
Was stealing a yard off some Quakers
An Elder named Halls
Just jumped on his balls
And gave him a couple of acres.

There was a young man from Llandinging
Who long kept the bed-springs a-pinging
The girl said: "Ooh Bevan
You said it was Heaven,
And now I can hear the harps ringing."

A girl engineer named Miss Holt
Had a foreman as spry as a colt
When she asked for a screw
What did the man do
But offer two nuts and a bolt.

There was a young lady loved salmon
She said to her boy: "Though I am on,
And I can't, as we wish
Have your fish in my dish
We can do just as well with some gammon."

Don was chokkers, to speak in vernacular
To find that Flo's flow was spectacular
She tried to be kind:
"Have a drink, never mind –"
"Flo! My name is Donald, not Dracula."

# You for Coffee?

The London–Manchester express train was crowded with business men.

In a first-class carriage a Chinaman was sitting reading quietly, when a white-coated waiter came down the corridor, put his head in the door and said:

"You for coffee?"

"No, you ferk offee, I got first-class ticket."

## HONEYMOON SALAD – LETTUCE ALONE

There was a waitress who went up to the Head Waiter and said:

"I'm not going to serve that cheeky devil over there!"

"Why not?"

"Well, he asked me for 'French Salad', and when I said, 'What's that?' the devil said, 'It's the same as any other salad, only you serve it without dressing'."

## TO FILL A GAP?

The Bishop came down to breakfast and said to his wife: "Any post?"

"Yes," she said, "there's a letter from the Rector of Little Crumpet, and you'd better read it, because it's upset me, it's disgusting!"

The Bishop unfolded the Rector's letter, and read:

*My Lord, my wife died suddenly yesterday and it is most urgent and important that you send a substitute for the week-end.*

## FINGERED HER ORGAN

There was a piano in the front room, where Mary did her courting.

One evening the young man called, and soon afterwards Mother thought she heard funny noises emanating. She put her head in, and said:

"Is everything all right?"

"It's nothing," said the young man, "only that she started to laugh and giggle when I began to play. . . ."

"Ah, yes," said her mother, "she always was ticklish."


## SPLITTING THE DIFFERENCE

There was a Chorus Master whose job in life was to train young girls for dancing acts in night clubs. He set on a new leading girl, who turned out to be stubborn and self-willed as well.

They were rehearsing a new show, and she wanted to dance topless, he wanted her in a see-through blouse, and a row was brewing up. Suddenly she stopped, and said: "Life's too short to quarrel, let's have a little contest – if I win, topless, if you win, see-through."

"Very well then, what's the competition?"

"Simple," said she, "we'll just see who can do the splits the best!"

"What, and you've got a start!"


## BAD AUSPICES?

There were two men in a bar having a fearful row about whether Burton beer was better than London beer. They were nearly coming to blows, so the landlord said: "Gentlemen, do not fight, simply lay your bets with me, and I'll send two samples to the County Analyst."

This was agreed upon, but unfortunately the covering letter went astray.

A crowded bar heard the landlord read the report: "I beg to assure you that neither of these women is pregnant."

# THE LAST TRUMP

There was an old maid went to the doctor, and complained that she was passing wind all day. The doctor, who was busy, said: "A lot of people do."

"Yes, Doctor, but mine is entirely odourless!"

He took notice, "Can you do it now?"

"Yes, indeed, I never stop."

The doctor looked concerned, and said an immediate operation was indicated.

"Oh dear, Doctor, on my backside?"

"No indeed Miss, on your nose."

# PERMISSIVE SOCIETY

Hodge and Giles were old friends who ran neighbouring farms. Hodge had a daughter, Giles a son. One fine evening Hodge walked over to Giles' place and after a long conversation about weather and crops, said:

"By the way, Garge, I ought to tell 'ee, I caught your lad lyin' on top o' Mary in th'ay loft larst night."

"Well, dammit, Tom! – there's a young devil, he'll be smokin' next!"

Nine months went by.

Again Hodge called on Giles. They discussed farm prices and the rotten government. As he turned to go, Hodge added:

"Oh, Garge, that there lad o' yourn, he have put my Mary in the pod."

"Oh, Tom, I dunno what to do wi' 'im 'e be gettin' so careless, only last week 'e broke a teacup."

## BACK TO THE LAND

Two London girls wanted badly to get work on a farm, and when the farmer asked them if they were experienced they rather misunderstood the question, and swore that they were.

"Very well," he said, "you can start. The cow's due for service, and the bull is being driven up in half an hour, so just get Bluebell ready for him, will you?"

With that, he went indoors for his dinner. Shortly there was a good deal of disturbance, which he ignored until the girls rushed in, with their clothes nearly torn off them.

"What be the matter then, for the lord's sake?"

"Oh farmer, it's Bluebell, we can't get her to lie on her back."

## A SORE POINT

There was a shapely farmer's daughter, sixteen, who had to drive her father's cow to another farm where the bull was kept. She put the cow in the yard, and the young labourer drove the bull in and shut the gate. The bull wasted no time, and as the labourer stood watching, beads of sweat came to his forehead: "By golly, I wish I was doing that," he said.

"Go on then," said the girl, "I'm not stopping you."

"No miss, but perhaps the cow wouldn't like it."

# ALL A LOT OF BULL

There was an old farmer, very set in his ways. When the bull died he tried to buy another, but everywhere he went he met with same response:

"No bulls for sale now, it's all this artificial insemination."

He didn't like to admit he didn't know what it was about, but finally, in desperation he rang up the A.I. centre and enquired about the drill.

When the Vet realised the farmer was a novice with A.I. he gave him some pretty strict instructions:

"I'll come next Monday and do it, and remember: I shall expect the cowshed well whitewashed and the floor scrubbed: I shall want hot water, soap and clean towels. . . ."

"Yes, Sir," said the farmer, "is that all?"

"And I shall not go near the animal unless she's spotlessly clean, understand?"

The farmer said he did understand. When the day came the farmer said to the Vet: "I've done arl ye said, I've got ye arl ye want, and I've put ye an 'ook, as well."

"A hook, a hook! What the hell would I want a hook for?"

"Well, Sir, I didn't think you'd want to throw your trousers down on the floor, even if it is clean."

# COULDN'T FATHOM IT OUT

An old sportsman had supported his local rugger club loyally for many years, but alas the Old Borstalians had a series of bad seasons, and became somewhat of a joke. As the old sportsman lay on his deathbed he sent for the Club Secretary.

"Jenkins," he said, "I've supported the club loyally, always coughed up the shekels when the hat came round, what!"

"Yes you have, Sir," said the Sec., "we'll miss you very much."

"Will you do me one last favour Jenkins, will you and the club come and stand for a few moments on my grave, in remembrance like?"

"Why of course, of course – where are you going to be buried?"

"At sea old boy, at sea!"

# HE PUT HIS FOOT IN IT!

The captain of a rugby club was much concerned because his best player was losing form, he asked what the trouble was?

The player explained that he was depressed because he was getting no sex life. The captain knew that this splendid athlete was very attractive to women, so he asked him why he didn't just go out and get it.

The player, after a great deal of humming and haa-ing, explained that he was a fetishist, and when it came to the point the girls cried off, because they would not let him put his number-ten-size foot in it.

The captain was a man of resource; he must get this man back into form, so he gave him ten pounds out of the kitty, and told him to go up the West End, where services, however kinky, were available for money.

\*   \*   \*

It had been a hard day at the hospital, and as the doctor sat down wearily to his tea, he said to his colleague: "You know Smithers, you never stop learning on this job, do you. Who would have thought that in one day I would have to treat a prossy with athletes foot in her fanny, and a big hulking footballer with syph in his great toe."

# SEX WITH KNOBS ON

A woman went to a solicitor and said she must have a divorce, owing to her husband's sexual demands. "Tell me?" said the man of law.

The wife explained that her husband wanted sex every night and twice on Sundays. "That's not unreasonable," said the solicitor.

"That's not all," she went on. "He takes me in the day time. I can't enter any room that he's in, but he rushes across for a stand-up job."

"My dear lady," said the lawyer, losing patience, "you are lucky to have a virile husband, and sexual intercourse up against a door is not grounds for a divorce."

"Oh, indeed!" said the woman, "then how would you like it if you had to keep going to hospital to have a brass doorknob removed from your backside?"

# THAT WAS THE WHOLE IDEA

It was a family wedding, the house was crowded with people, and at bedtime everybody had to "double up". A bridesmaid of sixteen, made randy by the occasion, was put to bed with a cousin a year older.

There was a deal of fidgetting, and the girl said: "Let's change sides, you roll over me, and I'll roll over you."

"Don't bother," said the lad, "I can just as easily get out and walk round."

This happened several times more, and the frustrated girl said:

"You know, I don't think you really understand what I want!"

"Oh yes, I do," he said, "you want the whole bloody bed, but you're not going to get it."

# HOT STUFF

Outside a West End cinema which was showing a film called "The Facts of Life" was a young man kicking an older man. A policeman came along to make an arrest, but the younger man explained that the older man had asked him to do it.

The older man then explained: twenty years ago he had been taken to the flat of a young woman who removed her jumper and skirt because she was too hot, and he had got up and turned off the gas fire. Then she took off her knickers and bra, upon which the man got up to go. As he left, she had said to him: "One day you will think about this, and you will ask the first man you meet to kick you."

"I've just found out what she meant," said the man.

"Kick him again," said the policeman.

# THE OAF AND THE LOAF

There was a country chap in London during the war stopped a passing girl and said he could not get a lodging.

"My husband's abroad," she said, "come home with me, a slice off a cut loaf is never missed."

"Sorry madam, you misunderstand me, it's a bed I'm looking for, not a meal."

## BACKS TO THE LAND

A man went to Russia to study the system. One day he was out in a peasant district, and he saw that the women toiled from morning to night in the fields. He spoke to one of the women and asked her if that was her idea of the "Communist paradise".

By this time a little group of interested bystanders had gathered, and the woman asked the man to explain what happened in Capitalist England. The man spoke good Russian, and he gave quite a fluent account: the men got up early, took their wives a cup of tea, and went off to work all day. At night they helped put the children to bed, and did any odd jobs about the house.

"There comrades," said the woman, "the Capitalist system is hell for the women, just as we were taught; it is a society in which all the men go to bed tired."

## ADJUSTABLE SCREW

A man was in the top bunk, of a cross-Channel steamer, and a young woman was in the lower bunk. The man peered over, and saw the girl remove her wig, false teeth, and glass eye. Then she unscrewed her artificial leg.

At that moment she realised the man was watching her, looked up angrily, and said:

"What are you waiting for?"

"Miss, you know damn well what I'm waiting for, hurry up and unscrew it, and throw it up here."

## DOWN MEMORY LANE

There was a dear old lady, who had been a widow for many many years.

One day a young married woman came visiting, bringing her baby. When she undressed the infant to bath it, she held it up for Grandma's inspection, and said:

"Isn't that a lovely baby?"

"Heh, heh, yes indeed it is, and, if my memory serves me rightly, a boy."

# OLD AGE WENCHIN?

A certain student was told to do research on "Problems of the Aged" so he went and consulted an expert on the subject.

The expert said: "Let us take the women first, over 70 they really don't need it for health, yet they often have a desire for it, and wish they could do it more often. Subject to their physical limitations, such as stiff legs, they may still be enthusiastic. Unfortunately, in most cases their husbands will by then have lost all interest.

"Although women lose their looks early, they often retain more physical vigour than men. Men, even men who have enjoyed it all their lives, men who have spent time and money on it, men who have given a lot of thought to looking after their equipment, don't seem to bother in old age, they would rather watch the telly."

CONCLUSION: "I conclude then," wrote the student, "that men and women over 70 tend to give up gardening."

# DOGGED DOES IT

An American entered a crowded railway carriage, but the only spare seat was occupied by a nasty alsatian, owned by a big red-faced woman in hunting tweeds. He asked if the dog might be put on the floor, and got the reply: "You leave the bloody dog alone!"

The Yank searched the train in vain for a seat, came back, and threw the dog out of the window.

"Are you going to stand by and let this wretched American do that to a gentlewoman?" she said to the carriage at large.

A man in a bowler hat lowered his *Times* and said: "The Yanks are always wrong, Miss; they eat with the fork in the wrong hand, they drive on the wrong side of the road, and now this fool's thrown the wrong bitch out of the window."

## NOT TRUSTWORTHY

There was a very keen businessman who met a friend in his club.

"How's trade?" said the friend.

"Trade's excellent, since I have set on a brilliant young accountant. Unfortunately he has seduced my daughter, put my cashier in the family way, and sexually assaulted my wife."

"That's bad Jock, that's bad, what are you going to do?"

"Going to do! I'm going to watch that bleeder like a hawk, and if I catch him fiddling the petty cash, I shan't hesitate, I shall sack him."

## WOULD NOT PLAY "POKER"

There were four passengers in the railway carriage, a young gentleman, a red-faced tycoon, a parson and the parson's wife.

The tycoon took out whisky and offered it the boy. "I don't drink, thank you," was the reply.

He took out cigars. . . . "I don't smoke," said the boy.

He took out a pack of cards. . . . "I never gamble," the young man replied.

As they left the train, the parson overtook the young man, and said:

"What a pleasure it is to meet a young man today, so entirely pure and free from sin. My wife here, and I, would like you to come down to our place for the weekend, and meet our charming daughter."

"Thank you," said the young man, "I'm a homo, on the run from the police."

## OATS AND BREAKFAST

A man lost in the country begged a lodging with a small-time farmer.

In the morning, he asked what he owed.

"I don't rightly know," said the farmer, "I aint never took anyone in afore. Let me see, there's your supper, and your bed, and your breakfast; then you screwed my wife once, and my daughter twice, do you think thirty bob would be asking too much?"

## LET US SPRAY

It was a crowded men's hairdressers. In one seat sat a retired Colonel, and the barber was saying: "Shall I spray a little scent on it Sir?"

"How dare you!" said the Colonel, "If I went home with that muck on my hair, my wife would say I smelled like a brothel."

Just then a private in the Pioneer Corps was asked the same question, by the barber at the next chair.

"Yes, a'course, spray me with all of 'em, my wife don't know what a brothel smells like."

## FOR SALE AND WANTED

A certain Bishop had heard that one of his city parishes was a nest of sin, so he went down one day to have a look round. The Vicar was away, but the Curate undertook to show him round, and off they went through the streets.

They had not gone very far when a girl passed by: high heels, short skirt, big white handbag, and loaded with make-up.

"Upon my soul!" said the Bishop, "what an eyesore."

A little further on two more tarts went by.

"Look my lord," said the Curate, "there are two more nice whores."

# CHEESED OFF

A man was getting very fresh with his girl in a railway carriage.

The only other occupant was an old shopkeeper who was sound asleep. Having wrecked the top-hamper the young man investigated the lower end. The girl protested that the old boy opposite might only be pretending to be asleep.

The bold young man said he would soon put the matter to the test, and stuck his fingers under the grocer's nose.

The old man shuffled in his sleep, and murmured, "Gorgonzola".

# HE DID NOT RISE TO THE OCCASION

A man and a woman were alone in a railway carriage on a long journey.

The train passed through farmland, and at one point they observed a boar mounting a sow. A bit further on they observed a stallion mounting a mare. Next it was a bull serving a cow.

The woman, who was getting more and more restless, told the man she was unmarried, and wanted to know more about it.

The man, who was a professor, said it would be a pleasure to educate her in the facts of life. He then spoke at great length about the female heat cycle, and how it led to certain odours, and these olfactory indications produced libido in the male, etc., etc.

When they parted as the train reached Euston, he said, he hoped he would meet such a charming lady again.

"Only when your cold in the head is better," she said.

## WRESTLING WITH SIN?

A young man boasted to his friend that he was courting a smashing bit of crumpet. The next time they met the young man had a black eye.

"How come you got that black eye?"

"Well," explained the other, "I was harmlessly dancing in the parlour with my girl to music from the radio. Her father walked in, and it turned out he was absolutely stone deaf."

## TOPPED AND TAILED

Two factory girls, friends, were talking.

"What's become of that nice fellow you started going out with Mary?"

"Oh, I gave him the push, he was no gentleman."

"What happened?"

"No sooner were we alone on the settee in the front room when he put his hand up my thighs."

"Well, that shows interest, anyway."

"Oh no, I was brought up proper, I'm not having that, every lady knows that with a real gentleman it's always tits first."

## THREW THE TOWEL IN

A man was in an upper bunk on a cross-Channel steamer. In the bunk below were a honeymoon couple. Every time the steward passed by, the groom said: "Steward, bring two towels."

After this had happened six times the man in the upper bunk shouted:

"Steward, bring me one towel, and some sleeping tablets."

# FRIGHTENING EXPERIENCE

A girl asked her mother what would happen on her wedding night. The mother was old-fashioned and prudish. She said: "Well, he'll take you to bed, and strip all the clothes off you. Then he'll undress, and lie on you, and . . . er, scare you, but you'll have to put up with it."

After the first time the bride looked up coyly, and said: "Darling, scare me again." This was repeated several times more.

When they woke up in the morning the bride at once said: "Darling, scare me again."

The groom opened his bleary eyes, slowly drew in a breath, and said: "Boo!"


# ARTIFICIAL INSEMINATION

There was a woman and a little boy sharing the top bunk in a steamer.

No sooner were they in bed than Willy told his mother he must get down and have a wee-wee. It was a long way down, and while mother was wondering how the kid would get back, he reappeared.

"How did you get up so easily, Willy?"

"Mother I put my foot on the bare bum of the man in the bottom bunk."

"Did you indeed, and what did he say?"

"He didn't say anything, but a lady's voice called out 'thankyou'."


# WASTE OF POLLEN

A girl student was alone in a train with a boy student. He persuaded her to fondle him, but in case the guard should come by, she did it under a piece of fancy wrapping paper. They both fell asleep. The paper blew down on to the floor.

The guard came along, woke the girl up, and said: "Excuse me, Miss, your bouquet has wilted."

A hospital Sister named Dabbitts
Was noted for slap-happy habits,
Mixing pills for sterility
With those for fertility
Had ten at a birth, plus some rabbits.

He made such a hullaballoo
At finding no "roll" in the loo
That his mother said: "Ted
You've a tongue in your head!"
"Ma! I'm not a giraffe at the Zoo."

A champion swimmer named Last
Was noted for making love fast,
He'd start at the rude end
By grabbing the pudend
And leave the breast-stroking 'till last.

A snob Tory filly at Kew
Wore Union Jack briefs in full view,
Some Communist shirkers
Cried: "Up with the workers
And down with the red white and blue!"

There was a young lady of Eton
Whose figure had plenty of meat on
She said: "Marry me, Neal
And have a good meal,
I can't cook, but I'll get you a 'Beat-on'."

# Right Upper Entrance

An old broken-down actor was signing-on for months at the Labour Exchange, and they were sick of him. One day the clerk said: "I'm sending you for a job, and you'd better keep it, or we'll cancel your benefits."

"What's the job?" enquired the old stager.

The clerk explained it was dead easy, it was to be prompter and assistant stage manager for a West End show that was being rehearsed.

The next day the man was back.

"What's your story? and it had better be bloody good, or you've had it," said the clerk sharply.

The actor explained that it was all on account of the Leading Lady being a prude, and the chorus girls having low blouses and low minds.

"Cut the cackle," said the clerk sharply, "and get on with it."

"Well," said the failed prompter, "I called out during rehearsal: *Enter the Duchess with a candle right up her entrance,*' the girls giggled, and the Director said: 'That can't be right, try again' so I started again, and read out, *Enter the Duchess with a candle left upper entrance.* At that point the Duchess swore, the chorus girls laughed until their tits fell out, and I got me bleeding cards."

## SHE WOULD BE TORPEDOED

The troopship was crossing the Indian Ocean, and the Major was as randy as hell. He had his eye on the ship's nurse, who was as shapely as she was prudish. However he was a bold warrior, and although it took him a week to get the top button undone, he persisted. With only two more weeks to go, he thought seriously of taking the last bastion by storm, and planting his standard between the ramparts, but his nerve failed.

Alas, the ship got torpedoed, and while the captain was giving emergency orders, the Major appeared on the bridge, and said:

"Is the ship sinking?"

"Oh suck off, I'm busy, what's the matter, are you scared?"

"Not at all, Sir, but if we're going to sink I propose to use the last five minutes making up that bitch's mind for her!"

## PAYMENT IN KIND

A theatrical Director was casting a play, and was interviewing a string of "starlets". When one came in whose breasts and backside were pleasing to him, he said she could have a small part if she took off her clothes and got down on the carpet. He had not finished the sentence before she was ready.

Not having wasted any time on finesse, he soon refastened his trousers and said: "Right, rehearsals three months tomorrow."

"Good God!" she said, "three months, I'm starving, can't you advance me a couple of quid to buy food?"

"Miss, do not be offensive, I am not a shop-keeper, and I do not buy sex either, I am a Director, I give free passes."

## SAFETY IN NUMBERS

A young man was desperately in need of sex, but he soon found that although respectable girls would never sell sex, they expected expensive presents.

He had little money, but plenty of brains, and he told this typist he would buy her an expensive fur coat if she cared to be cooperative.

In no time at all she was naked on the bed, and so was he.

Afterwards he gave her his card, and told her to go to the furriers and take her choice. "If there's any question," he said, "tell them to phone me at this number."

"Is it your home or your office?" she enquired.

"Actually, it's the sweet shop on the corner, but they'll call me."

## STOP IT I LIKE IT

Girl and boyfriend, having a row:

He: "I'll come up tonight and I'll tear the clothes off your back."

She: "Oh no you won't!"

He: "Then I'll do you and do you till you can't get up off the floor."

She: "Oh no you won't!"

He: "And I won't even wear a french letter."

She: "Oh yes you will!"

# HOLE FULL OF SOAP

There was a beautiful and shapely young girl married to an actor, who was mostly "resting". One day she told him that if he didn't get a job and bring some money in, she would leave him for a rich sugar daddy.

The upshot was, she had to sleep with a Director to get her spouse a part, and she told him he'd better be good at it, or else. . . .

It was one of those romantic plays which opened with a beautiful young girl lying on a bank in summer, in a frail dress, wafted by a gentle breeze.

He had to come on as a love-lorn prince, and say:

> *Ah, she sleeps, and dreams of peace*
> *Her soul is full of hope.*
> *So shall I quickly snatch a kiss,*
> *And fly off in the air.*

Now, being very nervous he had taken several snifters before going on, and by bad luck the "gentle breeze" had blown up the dress, revealing nothing underneath except perhaps a little barber's rash. He declaimed:

> *Ah, she sleeps and dreams of a piece*
> *Her hole is full of soap.*
> *So shall I quickly kiss her snatch*
> *And shoot off in the air.*

# PULLING THE BELLE

There was a college chap and a college girl, returning from a football game. They were rather excited as their team had won, and the girl suggested they stop the car in the woods, and get against a tree for a little smooching.

The man didn't like to admit that he'd never done it before, and when he'd finished he said: "Darling, I suppose you must have enjoyed it a lot, as you kept nodding your head?"

"As a matter of fact Charles, you'd got my scarf tucked in as well."

# FAST AND LOOSE

A woman went to Court and demanded a divorce. After a lot of beating about the bush it came out that her husband's member was so big that it really hurt. The divorce was granted.

A year later she was back. She had remarried, and this time she wanted a divorce because her husband's was so tiny it could not satisfy her.

"Case dismissed!" roared the Judge. "Madam, the Court has better things to do than fitting dicks to your vagina."


# PUDDING WITH SAUCE

Father was talking to Mother: "You know, I'm not altogether happy about our Mary getting engaged, I hear the chap's a vegetarian."

Mother: "Well if the chap's a vegetarian, it's just not on, we don't want any cranks and weirdies in our family."

Little sister Jane, who was seven, had been listening quietly, and now asked: "What's a vegetarian?"

"A man who will never eat meat."

"Oh, that's all right then."

"What do you mean dear 'that's all right'?"

"Well, yesterday, when I peeped into the front room through the keyhole he was making a good meal off our Mary's tits."

# SHE SAW THE DRAWBACK

A respectable high-class Jewish family were at dinner, and Father said to Mother: "By the way, I hear Emmanuel wants to join that Nudist Club down the road."

"I can't really think of any objection," said Mother.

"Mother!" said the thirteen-year-old daughter of the house, "our Manny can't possibly join that Club?"

"Why on earth not, my dear?"

"They're all gentiles!"

"How can you possibly know that, my child?"

"Daddy. Mummy, of course I know. I peeped through a crack in the fence."

## AN UPRIGHT OLD MAN

Little Jimmy was playing in the garden, and he pulled a worm out of its hole. Grandad was watching, and to tease little Jimmy, he said:

"I bet you half a crown you can't put it back!"

Little Jimmy said: "Oh yes I can, Grandad, you come back here in half an hour, and I'll show you!"

So, half an hour later, Jimmy reappeared with the worm, which was now as stiff as a pencil, and he threaded it back into its hole without much difficulty.

Grandad was amazed, and asked how it was done.

"Pay up the half crown you owe me, and I'll tell you," said the child.

Grandad handed over the money, and then Jimmy explained the trick. He had gone to his big sister's dressing-table, sprayed the worm with her hair varnish, and after a few minutes it was stiff and hard.

\* \* \*

The following day, Jimmy was again playing in the garden when his Grandfather came along and gave him half a crown. The boy was honest, and said:

"Grandad, you paid me yesterday."

"Yes, I know I did son, this one's from your Grandmother."

## CAUTIONARY TALE

Two young farm labourers were mowing the hay when they came across two girl cyclists from the city, picnicking in the grass. They told the girls they would have to pay damages for flattening the hay, but, after a bit of talk, the girls suggested paying on their backs. The boys were only too ready, but the girls produced condoms, saying: "You must wear these to prevent disease."

Two weeks later Herbert said to George: "You got any disease Garge?" – "No, Bert."

"Noither 'ave Oi, let's take these darn things off."

# COME BACK TO ERRING!

Pat grew up in a remote parish in Ireland, and he came to an understanding with a local colleen. But first he must go to America to establish himself, and he was gone ten years.

Pat returned, city-suited, pockets jingling, to the one-roomed sheiling where his girl's family lived. Naturally he had to stay the night, so he and Father went up to the "bedroom", which was no more than a sort of loft reached by a ladder, while the two women stayed below.

The men were not comfortable, and they lay awake listening to the mother and daughter whispering below:

"Well me darlin', ye'll soon be married now."

"Muther, you know I can't marry him. Have I not had a child, and it put out to adoption whiles he's away!"

Mother pooh-poohed all this, she said he'd never know, shut up about it.

"But mother, I must tell him, it's not honest."

"My child, my dear daughter, did I not myself have a child before I met your father, and him none the worse for not knowing on't?"

\* \* \*

Up aloft there was some shuffling; "Move over will ye," says Pat to father, "and let me get out of the ventilation hole, for am I not off back to Americky this minnit."

"Steady Pat, steady, whin ye get down, bring over the ladder from the hayrick, for it's meself that's coming wid ye."

# NO "R" IN THE MONTHLY

There was a shapely young woman went to the doctor because she was not too well. He took a sample of her water and told her to return later.

When the lady came back, he said: "Congratulations Mrs Brown, I have some good news for you. . . ."

"But Doctor, I'm MISS Brown."

"Then Miss Brown, I have some bad news for you."

## PENETRATED

A well set up widow of 38 had a daughter of 18. Mother considered herself of superior class, and had a very icy manner. She was quite pleased when her daughter started to go out regularly with the curate.

After some months she said to the daughter: "When are you getting engaged?"

"I'm not getting engaged Mother. We had a row and broke it off a fortnight ago."

"Oh indeed, and did you give him his ring back?"

"Yes I did, the horrible beast, and I secretly made pin-holes in those french letters he was proposing to use on me . . . oh Mother, you've fainted!"

## UP WITH THE WORKERS

A young porter in an hotel was brought up in Court for raping the chambermaid. She alleged that while she was leaning out of the hotel window to watch a May Day parade, the youth lowered the sash, trapped her, and took his will of her.

"But Miss," said the Judge, "why didn't you start yelling?"

"What, and have everybody thinking I was supporting the Labour Party!"

## HANDS UP EVERYBODY

Bandits held up a holiday coach at gun point on a wild and lonely moor. The chief bandit cried: "Right, stand fast, we're going to rob all the men and do all the women."

"Boss," said his assistant, "wouldn't it be safer to rob all the men and then get to hell out of it?"

An old maid at the back: "Who's in charge of this robbery I should like to know."

## THAT WON'T WASH

A young man was courting for the first time, and it wasn't
long before he got the girl undressed. But she wouldn't let
him without a sheath, and he didn't know what they were.
"Any chemist will explain," she told him.

So off he went, and the chemist said they were half a
crown each, but it was much better to buy ten-shilling ones,
because these could be washed and used again.

Some time later he met the chemist in the street, who
asked him if he was having any luck with the lady. "That
part was OK," he said, "but I got a hell of a stinking note
from the manager of the laundry."

## THUMBS UP

A chap was making pretty good progress with a girl. She
agreed to go away for the weekend, provided he brought a
sheath with him.

When they went upstairs to bed, he admitted he didn't
know how to wear it, so she rolled it down his thumb to
show him. Then they put the light out and got on with it.

After a while the girl said: "You know I'm terribly
sticky, I do believe you've broken that thing."

"Oh no I haven't," he said, and (switching the light on)
"here it is, still on my thumb."

# BLINDED WITH SCIENCE

A man was determined to fail his army "medical" on the grounds of semi-blindness. When the doctor said: "Read that card," he said: "What card?" "The card on the wall, man!" – "What wall doctor?"

The doctor indicated to the shapely nurse to strip naked.

"Now, what do you see?" – "The figure 8," said the man, so he was discharged. He was so pleased he rushed up town and went to a Strip Club. When the lights came up at an interval, who should be sitting in the next seat but the doctor who had just failed him. Quick as a flash, he said:

"This is the bus for Charing Cross, isn't it Miss?"

# NOBLESSE OBLIGE, BUT NOT TONIGHT

There was a dashing young man, the son of a Peer, who went to a Deb's coming-out ball. The band played, the champers went round, and all was merry. Young Fitznakkers was smitten by a bird whose dress was open down to her navel, and after turning on the old charm he had little difficulty in getting her on a couch in the conservatory, well hidden behind some shrubbery.

Such was his progress that pretty soon her pants and bra were decorating the branches. He was nearly there, when she cried off:

"No no, Charles, that's enough, stop now."

He was in no condition to put the brakes on: "Darling, darling, don't be frightened, this is real love, darling: will you marry me?" (At that moment he really meant it.)

"No darling, I won't. I love you, but I must say No now."

He was obliged to make love to his best silk handkerchief, after which, feeling a little calmer, he fetched some drinks and said:

"Darling, I offered honourable marriage; you love me and I love you, yet you said No."

"You see, Charles," she explained, "it's an old family superstition."

"Old family superstition, what the hell are you on about?"

"Well, you see, my father proposed to my mother in the conservatory, and he died the same night."

# THE BRIDE WANTED COVERING

There was a charming and beautiful young girl went on honeymoon with her dashing husband. She went up to bed first to get ready, and he followed soon afterwards. He found her starkers in the bedroom, except for a small beret on her head.

"Darlingest pet," he said, "have you gone crackers?"

"No, Harry darling, I'm just following my mother's good advice; I don't know what she meant, but I'm sure she must have had good reason."

"Why duckiest, what did she say?"

"She said, if I wanted to keep my husband's interest I must never let him see me totally naked."

# A DIFFERENT SORT OF RIDE

A chap was up before the Bench for stealing a young woman's bicycle. He pleaded "Not guilty".

"Well, what happened?" said the Beak.

"Well, Sir, I was walking through the woods and this girl came by on her bike and stopped, and she got me to sit down although I wasn't tired, then she took her blouse off, although it wasn't that hot, and then she said 'Kiss me'."

"Yes, go on."

"Well, Sir, I kissed her and she took her jeans off, then she took her panties off, then she said: 'Kiss me again and you can have what you like'."

"And then?"

"Well, Sir, panties is girls clothes, and her jeans wouldn't fit me, so I had her bicycle."

## PUT IT DELICATELY

There was a rough navvy up for burglary, but he seemed to have a reasonable alibi. Said the Judge: "Now tell us *everything* you did that night, in detail."

"Well, Sir, I comes 'ome for me *ing tea, and then I 'as a *ing wash and puts my *ing best shoes on. Then I goes up the *ing pub and I 'as several *ing pints, and in comes *ing Nelly. So I buys *ing Nelly a couple of *ing drinks, and takes her round the *ing back and across the *ing fields and into the *ing woods. Then I takes her *ing knickers off and lays her on the *ing ground, and. . . . Sir, I don't like to say any more, it ain't decent."

"Go on, go on," said the Judge, "if you want to stay out of jail, finish the story."

"Well, then we 'as sexual intercourse."




## HOLE IN ONE

There was a man went into a bar looking very cheerful, and he instantly called for "drinks on the House".

A stranger enquired what was the source of his joy, and the man said: "This morning my wife gave birth to a fine son, our eleventh, think of that, what a bit of luck!"

"I can't see it old boy, nothing but damned expense, surely?"

"Money doesn't worry me," said the happy father, "but I am a soccer fan, and now I can have a football team . . . more drinks! landlord."

There was a long pause, and the stranger, who had been melancholy, looked up suddenly with a smile, and said:

"No, these are on me, I've just thought of something."

The others enquired as to the source of his inspiration and were told:

"Well gentlemen, you know I've got seventeen daughters, if we have one more I'll have a golf course!"

A rather shy man was courting a passionate girl, and each time he visited her home she would make a point of going on the back porch with him as he departed. Little by little she was leading him on, and one night during an embrace he discovered there was nothing else under her dress.

His emotions began to stir, his breath was getting shorter, and finally he said:

"If I were to go all the way, would you yell for your mother?"

"Why!" said the girl, "do you want to do it to her as well?"

## NICER THAN PORK?

A factory Welfare Officer was visited by a weeping girl.

"Usual trouble, I suppose?"

"Yes, Miss."

"Married man, I suppose?"

"Yes Miss."

"Here! Aren't you Fanny Hitches who came to me in the same pickle just a year ago?"

"Yes, Miss."

"You stupid little fool, what did you go and do it again for?"

"Well, Miss, if God made anything nicer, you tell me what it is."

# CLOSED SHOP

There was a man who was his mother's pet. He didn't get married until he was thirty. "I've brought him up to be choosey," his mother would say.

When he did get married he returned to his mother the next day.

"Why have you left her, Dear?" said Mam.

"I found out she was a virgin, Mother."

"What's the objection to that, son?"

"Well, Mother, if she's not good enough for the lads of the village, she's not good enough for me."


# IT GOT UP HER PIPE

Prewar Council houses were not well built. A woman went to her neighbour on the "estate" and said:

"Hey, Mrs Bloggs, have you got the sweep in?"

"What if I has then," replied the other, cautiously.

"This is what, Mrs Bloggs, you just tell him to be a damn sight more careful what he's a-doin'. He's pushed our Johnny off the lavatory twice with his brush."

A honeymoon pair from Nantucket
Went to bed, and by heck, did they ruck it!
Next morning, said he:
"Do you feel like some tea?"
"No! I feel like a billposter's bucket."

A lockkeeper's daughter named Baines
Sobbed: "Loss of virginity pains,
An artist," she said:
"Came through Maidenhead
Whose brushwork left nothing but Staines."

An Ordnance Surveyor of guile
His ranging rod used in such style
That in taxis the sod
Put virgins in pod
On the scale of one inch to one mile.

A certain blonde rider named Hatch
Withdrew from the Hunt with despatch
When she fell at some ditches
And ruptured her britches
The hairs on her brush didn't match.

There was a girl student named Grubb
Too young to be served in a pub,
Said a Yorkshire churchwarden:
"Just come in the garden,
Ah'll serve thee, and put thee in Club."

# Custer's Last Stand

In the prairie where Custer made his famous last stand against the Sioux there now stands a prosperous town, and the City Fathers held a meeting. They had to decide what they would do to celebrate the hundredth anniversary of this great piece of American history.

After due debate it was decided to put up ten thousand dollars and engage the best painter they could find to paint a huge mural for the Town Hall, depicting the event.

Picasso was suggested.

"Mister May-yor, ain't he just a bit . . . wal, he's French I guess," said one. "That guy sure paints hot noods," said another. "Wid square boobs!" added a third.

"Sure, sure," said the Mayor, "but fer ten grand we can tie him down like to a prarper picture."

It was agreed that Picasso should have the contract if he would undertake to do a lifelike historical record with no abstract stuff. It was to demonstrate the drama of the scene so that simple cowboys could grasp it.

Picasso had this drummed into him, and at the same time he insisted that the great work should remain under cover until finished.

**\*   \*   \***

When the great day came, hundreds were packed into the hall, including all the big-wigs of the city, county and state. The President sent a message.

A Senator's wife pulled a silk cord, and the drapes fell off, revealing a giant canvas covered all over with naked Indians. The crowd gasped to see that each Indian brave was coupled frankly with a squaw wearing only a head-dress. The detail was marvellous! In the top corner was a fish with a halo over it.

The Mayor turned to Picasso and heaped abuse on him. Picasso mumbled in French. . . . "How in heck does he allow this to hev anny rellervance to Ammurican history?" demanded the Mayor of the interpreter.

*cont'd over*

The interpreter questioned Picasso, and then said: "He makes it out like this Mister May-yor – he says how he's checked up on Custer's very last words on earth. . . . HOLY MACKEREL! LOOK AT ALL THEM ****ING INDIANS!"


HOSPICE

The Women's Institute had a "Men's Night" and all the ladies had to bring their husbands, willing or unwilling.

To liven the proceedings, a "spelling bee" was laid on, and to everyone's surprise, Old Farmer Haycock was out in front of the field.

Indeed, as he said in the Barley Mow afterwards: "Ar, and I'd a-won it an arl, if the last word hadn't been 'Auspices'."

# NOT YET WRITTEN OFF

There was an Army P.T. instructor who finished his time out in the Far East. To the disappointment of his family he did not come back to England but took a job out there.

His Dad wrote several times to ask him what the job was, but he always evaded the question. At last he came home on a long vacation, and his Dad took him out for a few drinks. "Now Jack," he said, "out with it, what's this job you're doing?"

The son explained he had a really well-paid number at the court of one of these wealthy oil sheiks.

"Yes, but WHAT?"

"Well, Dad, it's a kind of educational job."

"Educational! Why you bloody ignoramus you were always bottom of the class. Come on, out with it, trust your old Dad."

Jack said: "Well, it's like this here, I has a wall painted black, and I gets sent a lot of well-made fourteen-year-old virgins from the villages, see, and I has to teach them arithmetic, see."

"Do you mean to say you get a fancy salary for that?"

"Well hang on a minnit, Dad, it ain't that easy, it takes perseverance see, but when they pass out trained the Boss is very satisfied."

"What do they have to do to pass out?"

"When they can hold a stick of chalk in the cheeks of their arse, and write one and seventeen-thirtyseconds plus three and twentynine-sixtyfourths equals four and sixtythree-sixtyfourths on the wall, they're ready for the Sultan's harem, see."

# A POPULAR GIRL

There was a man who had got on only by his own efforts and made some money. He crowned his success by marrying a debutante of snooty extraction. On the wedding night she told him that she was too modest to undress in front of him, would he stay down, smoke a cigar, and have a final drink, then she would be ready. Actually he did not wait very long, but soon went after her.

When he entered his bedroom his wife was naked on the bed. Two bellboys were sucking her breasts, the night porter was on top, and she was gamming the boots.

"Oh, Delia," he said, "I am surprised!"

"But dahrling, why? I told you I was a bit of a flirt."

# SLIPPING THEM IN

A young woman was about to get married, and she was quite innocent. Her mother said: "Before you go to bed the first night, be sure and give him some oysters for supper."

Next day, mother asked daughter how she got on.

"Not very successful mother, I suppose it's because I lack your catering experience. I fed him a dozen, but only nine worked."

# BEST OF BOTH WORLDS

Two experienced women were talking. One said she had been in the East where male organs were short and thick, and she preferred them that way.

The other said she had always lived in the West where the male equipment was long and thin.

The daughter of one of them, who was not supposed to be listening, told her mother afterwards that she hoped to marry a man who had been in the Diplomatic Service.

"But why, my dear?"

"Then I might hope to find a man born in the West who had lived in the East a long time."


# YOU OUI-OUI OFF!

A working chap won the pools, so he and his wife set out for a holiday in Paris. They went out for a drink, and by chance wandered into Charrington's famous "English Pub".

The working man took out his phrase book and said:

"Voulay vouz donner moi a pint of beer, silver plate."

The waiter said: "Sorry, Sir, no French spoken here."

"Ho, you don't speak bloody French hey, well clear off and come back with the bugger that does."

## OVER TO METRIC

On the first day of each month a young man went into a chemist's shop, as regularly as clockwork, and ordered one gross of french letters. Recently the chemist said to him:

"Our industry's gone over to Metric, they come in packets of fifty now, not in dozens, actually it comes out slightly cheaper."

Customer: "Three packets of fifty?"

Chemist: "That's what I said, instead of a gross."

"What do you think I am, a sex maniac?"

## OLD RUGBY CUSTOMS

A parson went to his first rugby match. Shortly an excited scrum-half hacked an opponent's leg.

The parson turned to his friend, and said: "Excuse me, but how did that one player know the other player was a Bar steward?"

There was a girl, daughter of a noble house, who had breeding, but no money to go with it. At last she picked up with the son of a Duke, and an engagement was announced.

However, there was trouble, the girl went to her mother, and said:

"Charles says that if he finds I'm not a virgin on our wedding night, he'll make no settlement on me, and we'll all be ruined."

"You should have kept your virginity dear, shouldn't you."

"Dammit, I did keep it until I was eighteen, *you* sent me to Roedean!"

"That's no help now, we'll go and see Doctor Duguid."

The old family doctor shook his head. "When I was a student we weren't taught how to re-fabricate maidenheads. Anyway, it isn't necessary . . . (turning to the girl) this is the oldest trick in the world: go in the bathroom on your wedding night, and dry your orifice out with cotton wool. When your husband, half drunk anyway, gets going, scream the place down." (The girl shook her head.) "I tell you Miss de Hardwick, thousands of men have been taken in like that."

"Doctor, in the first place I'm a rotten actress, in the second, as soon as a man puts his hand on it, it runs like a tap. You'll have to think again."

"Well," said the doctor, "there's a Harley Street chap who was at college with me. . . ." ". . . We haven't got Harley Street money," said Mother.

"Then I'll do a local job for £25, it may work, Miss de Hardwick, come to me the day before."

\* \* \*

*cont'd over*  141

The wedding was not only a great social success, but the screams of the virgin bride disturbed the whole hotel. Mother went to pay the doctor his £25, and said, "It was good value for money, what did you actually do?"

"Well, Mrs De Hardwick, I sat up all night with the old books, but it was no good. Then I suddenly remembered I'd been in the Sea Scouts as a lad."

"And what, may I ask, have the Sea Scouts to do with restored maidenheads?"

"Why, I simply knotted the hairs together."


## DELAYED ACTION

Two elderly men met in a bar. They had been soldiers together, and got talking: "How are you getting on?" says one.

"Not very well," says the other, "you know that dope the medical officer used to put in the troops' tea to quieten us down?"

"Yes, what about it?"

"It's just beginning to catch up on me."

## DOUBLE MEANING

There was an irritable businessman used to play golf, with his wife. One day a visiting niece of fifteen went round with them. The golfer misses a six-inch putt for the match, and shouts: "Oh f**k!"

The wife is shocked, and soundly rebukes her husband. The man looks at the girl, her full bust, her round bottom, her red lips, and says:

"Surely you must have heard that expression before?"

"Yes, Uncle, but not spoken in anger."


## IN A SHROUD

A policeman shone his torch into a graveyard late at night, and saw a courting couple making love. He brought them before the Judge:

"And what were you doing in the churchyard at midnight?" said the Judge to the young man.

"Nothing wrong, Your Honour, just burying a stiff."

"What about you?" he said to the girl.

"Your Honour, I was the undertaker."


## MISUNDERSTANDING

A middle-aged motorist and his wife could not find the country pub at which they were booked, and their petrol was running low.

"We can't go much farther," said the wife, when they were in the middle of nowhere, "there's a car in that spinney, go and see if you can get any directions."

The man went across, and came back with a black eye.

"All I did," he said, "was walk across to this couple, and call through the quarter-light: 'How far is the Cock Inn?' "

# THE MISCARRIAGE TRADE

A farmer had a plain thin daughter, and one day it turned out she was pregnant. The farmer loaded his shotgun and said: "He'll marry you or else. . . ."

"He's married already," said the girl. "It was the Squire."

Father said he'd shoot him just the same, and sallied off to the Hall in a frenzy.

"Here! hold on a minute Hodge old chap," said the Squire, "I mean to do right by the girl. If she has a boy, I'll settle a thousand quid on him, and if it should be a girl, five hundred quid."

"And if it's twins, Squire."

"Fifteen hundred. Now sod off you old blackmailer."

"Excuse me, Squire, just a final word: if it's a miscarriage, can she have another go?"

# SHE HAD EXPECTATION

A man of good family had gone abroad to complete his education, but unfortunately squandered all his money in brothels and casinos. He came home broke, and his father said: "Don't look at me, you'll just have to buy a business, if you can raise the dough. Try your Uncle George, he's rich."

The young man went to see Uncle George and said any chance of a loan of ten thousand? "No," said uncle, "I want my cash to marry my daughter off, hey, you'll do. Listen, she's got nice hair, a fine pair of tits, a well-shaped bottom, good teeth, a generous nature, a dowry of ten thousand, and all my expectations."

"And I'm penniless and unemployed!" said the cousin, "where's the catch, Uncle, out with it?"

"Well, my boy, I must confess that she is just the weeniest, teeniest bit pregnant."

## SHE PUT HER FEET IN IT

An Irish country woman went to the doctor and asked for some birth control pills. The doctor told her that it would be illegal in Ireland, and she said, with ten kids in ten years, and still only thirty years old, what should she do.

The doctor suggested she go back to the farm and cut the top off a two-gallon paraffin tin. If she slept with both feet in that every night, she would not become pregnant.

Six months later she was back, filled out in front. . . .

"I thought I told you. . . ."

"I know you did, Doctor, but you see, Pat buys his paraffin in one-gallon tins, so I put one on each foot."

## MEN OF CAPE HORN

A man went from town to town as a traveller in contraceptive goods.

He arrived at his regular hotel, and the reception girl said:

"Your regular room eh, Mr Smith?"

"No dammit, I want two rooms, one with three cots, and a bathroom, I've got three infants in the back of the car."

"Oh dear, has your wife suddenly run away?"

"Not at all, just going back to the factory with customers' complaints."

# UNLETTERED OAF

Two attractive girls moved down from college into a country town to open a chemists shop. A bold young man went in and asked for a packet of french letters. "What size, Sir?" – "I don't know."

"Well, go round the back for a fitting."

Round the back the other girl is waiting with her pants down: she slips it in, and shouts, "Size 6 Mary."

The man rushed round to tell his best friend, who at once set off on the same errand. When it came to trying for size however, the rotten hound left it in and came off.

"It's all right, Miss," he said to the furious girl, "I didn't come along to buy any, I just wanted a fitting."


# HAND IN GLOVE

A widow had a daughter who was rather innocent. The girl started courting, but one day out in the country the young man went over a hedge for a run out, and the girl peeped through to look, out of curiosity. Terrified by what she had seen, she ran home to mother and swore she could never marry.

Mother pooh-poohed this, and, after discussing it with the young man, it was agreed that they should have a trial run, so that the engagement could be broken off rather than a disastrous marriage be entered into.

Accordingly, the three of them retired upstairs on Saturday afternoon, and the sight of the girl's plump body roused the man to supreme heights. This in turn frightened the girl out of her wits, and she firmly closed her legs. Mother said: "Open them wide dear, and I will grasp him round the base of the stem, one hand above the other. Only if you can bear it will I remove one or both hands."

Operations commenced, and the mother very carefully removed one hand, and after a minute, the other. After five minutes the girl cried out:

"Mother, for cripes sake hurry up and take both hands away."

# VIRGIN BIRTH

A young and smarmy lawyer was up before the judge in a paternity case.

He had been actually seen swiving the girl at the relevant date, blood group tests were positive, and the judge could not wait to hear what sort of a case he would make in support of his plea of "Not Guilty".

"Well, my Lord, it's like this. This girl is nothing but a prickteaser. She would take me upstairs when her mother was out, lie naked on the bed, and then not let me put it in. At last she agreed that I could put the first inch in, if I stopped at the maidenhead. I kept my word like a true English gentleman; but on this occasion her mother came in unexpectedly, gave me a series of belts across the bare arse, and I went straight through and came off.

"My Lord, I submit that the father of the child is that girl's mother."

# THE OLD BAG

The daughter of a Welsh hill-farmer's family was being courted by a city fellow. One Saturday night there was a fearful storm, and then after that his motorbike wouldn't start, so there was no choice but for him to stay the night. This meant him sleeping in the daughter's bed, and mother was greatly troubled.

"Mother," whispered father, "look now is not the old bundling bag somewhere in grandad's trunk, go and look."

"Indeed to goodness yes," cried mother from the depths of the trunk, but alas, the upper half had been used for something else. So mother put Megan's feet and legs in the bag, tied it round her waist, and made her swear that she would in no circumstances get out of it.

\* \* \*

Several months later, Megan was pregnant. "Is it not a little liar that you are! Were you not swearing to me that you wouldn't get out of the bag?"

"But Mother, I didn't get out of the bag, at least, shall I put it this way Mother, only one leg."

# FIVE TIMES A VIRGIN

A young man was courting a Welsh girl who shared her family's narrow views. He tried drink, he tried gifts, he tried the top end and got encouragement, but when he tried the bottom end he found stout linen bloomers with elasticated legs.

She told him that never mind if the frustration was killing him, her mother would never let them share a bed unless a formal engagement was announced.

Buoyed with hope he bought a most expensive ring, and her parents put the pair of them to bed, but only in bundling bags with knots tied tight behind the neck.

He saw there was nothing to it but he would have to marry her. On the wedding night he said: "You know Olwen my dear, I'm just the same as other men, if you had let me have your virginity before, I wouldn't have been in a hurry to get married."

"I know," she said, "that's how I lost the other four."

# EMBARRASSING

A man in a pub was asked by a stranger if he'd got a light.

He said: "I'm a non-smoker, but I've got a match somewhere." With which he turned out all his pockets and produced six packets of aspirins and a quarter of cough lozenges.

"What's the matter mate, you got flu or something?"

"Not at all, it's every time I go into a chemists shop lately, they only seem to have women behind the counter."

## RED LETTER DAY

A man was cycling past a house in a narrow street when a used french letter was thrown out of an upper window, and hit him smack in the eye.

As this caused him to take a nasty tumble from the bike, he was very angry, and knocked at the front door of the house. Father came to the door, paper in hand, feet in slippers, and said: "Are you trying to break my door knocker?"

"Never mind that, who's upstairs where that light is?"

"My daughter, as a matter of fact."

"And who is with her?"

"My intended son-in-law, and what business is it of yours?"

"None at all my dear Sir, none at all, but I thought you would like to know that your intended grandson has just been thrown out of the window."

## HE WAS FABRIC-ATED

A man at work was very little, and although he had spent a long lifetime there, he was still teased because of his small size.

The day came when he had to put away his broom, and the directors gave a dinner, and Tich drank far more than he was used to. When it came to the speeches the Chairman said: "Now, before I ask my younger daughter to present our retiring labourer with this splendid gold watch, I am going to ask him if he cares to tell us how it is that he is so small."

"As to that," replied Tich, "I was born before french letters was invented." This produced such a shocked silence that he took it for encouragement. ". . . my mother made my father use his handkerchief, and you'd be little if you'd been strained through fine silk."

## SHE WAS ONLY AN ADMIRAL'S DAUGHTER ...

She was only an Admiral's daughter, but she loved a navel encounter, with a great loss of semen.

* * *

She was only the Mayor of Birmingham's daughter, but she knew Five Ways.

* * *

She was only a cardsharper's daughter, but she covered my jack with her deuce.

* * *

She was only a Huntsman's daughter, but all the horse-manure.

* * *

She was only a doctor's daughter, but she liked being bad in bed.

* * *

## ENLARGEMENTS WANTED?

There were some explorers pushing up through the jungle where no white man had ever been before. At last they broke through to the bank of a river where some native girls were bathing, together with a naked black man who had the largest chopper ever seen. This massive zeppelin was unique, and they asked through the interpreter if they could photograph it for the Science publications.

There was some mumbling, and then the interpreter returned and said:

"He wants to know what all the fuss is about. Does not the member of the white man shrink in cold water?"

# VENTILATED THE PROBLEM

There was a coloured man in Britain whose wife was having
so many children that the District Nurse persuaded him to
visit a doctor. The doctor, not without difficulty, got
through to him that he must wear a sheath. So long as he
wore it, his wife could not conceive.

However, she soon conceived again, and the doctor was
furious. He had the man in, and this time he laid on an
interpreter, through whom he questioned the man.

"He swears he did wear it, he never took it off," said the
interpreter.

"Then how the hell did his wife conceive, ask him that?"

"He says that after a week he was dying for a pee, so he
cut the end off."

# LIMERICKS VIII

There was a great swimmer named Hidges
Whose bottom got bitten by midges
To avoid the attack
He swam on his back
But his hampton got bashed on the bridges.

There was an old whore of Madras.
Who was bushed with a liner of brass
She would tinkle like hell
When they clappered the bell
And play the bass notes with her ass.

There was a young lady named Myrtle
Who would have it straight up or turned turtle
She littered a child
By the late Oscar Wilde
To prove to the world she was fertile.

There was a young lady named Laws
Who worked in a furniture stores
If rich clients pressed
On her very fine chest
She would readily open her drawers.

There was a shy virgin named Grace
Who said: "If the whole human race
Depends upon what
The boys call a twat,
Then it's put in a damned awkward place!"

# Fed Up, Fogged Up, and Far From Home

There was a rugby captain who became so weak they dropped him, and the trainer sent him to the psychiatrist, who asked him all about his dreams. "I have the same dreadful dream every night," said the patient. "I dream I am in the Strand with a barrow full of bricks, and I have to wheel them to Bethnal Green; I wake up completely beggared."

Said the Head Shrinker: "I know I can help you, take one of these pills each night when you go to bed, and that'll be ten guineas please."

The rugby captain took a pill at bed-time, and he had exactly the same dream as before, except that when he got as far as the Mile End Road the psychiatrist met him, took the barrow of bricks from him, and pushed them to Bethnal Green. Thus the man woke up much less exhausted, recovered his strength, and his place in the XV.

The good news went round the club, so that when the full back began to lose form they sent him at once to the same man.

"Explain your dreams," said he.

"Well, Doctor, I dream every night I am in a Sultan's harem. Ten fantastic girls come in, with breasts like melons, big thighs, pink round bottoms. . . ." "Yes-yes," said the quack, "never mind that, what do YOU do?"

"That's just it! One after another they demand my services, I get so I can't refuse, and I wake up shattered and shugged out."

After paying the fee, and taking the pills, he got worse instead of better.

"What's gone wrong?" said the trainer.

"Well, now, when I dream about the ten luscious girls the psychiatrist always arrives to take five of them off me. A rugger man of my age can manage five a night without bother, but, oh dear, when I finish and go outside, I find I am in the Mile End Road with a barrow full of bricks which I have to wheel to Bethnal Green!"

# MY KINGDOM FOR A HORSE'S

An enterprising young journalist was always on the lookout for "stories" and one day he read under "Legal Notices" that a Vet and a surgeon had formed a business partnership.

He thought there must be something unusual behind this, and he went round to the address given. Nobody answered the bell, but the door was open, so he pushed through to the back. Looking through a glass door he beheld a remarkable sight. There was a wealthy middle-aged man stretched out naked on an operating table, and he had a very shrivelled-up member. Nearby, on a huge slab, was a stallion under anaesthetic. The young journalist listened at the door, and he heard the surgeon say to the vet:

"You know, Jones, if we can only pull off this particular transplant, we shall both make our bloody fortunes."

# NEEDED FRESH HAIR?

There was a boastful young man, who thought he knew all the answers.

He married a girl who knew she knew all the answers.

They went on a Winter honeymoon in Oslo, when the nights were fourteen hours long.

After the bridal night the groom got up, stretched himself and boasted:

"Well, I feel like a new man now."

"So do I," said the bride.

## THE PRIMROSE PATH

There was a little girl whose parents brought her up "modern".

One day she was at a wedding, and when the bride and groom came out of the church and stood ready to be photographed, there was a bit of a hush.

Then a little girl's voice piped up: "Mummy dear, will he give her his pollen now, or wait 'til they get home?"


## LONG TIME PASSING

There was a methodical German, a passionate Frenchman, and a cold Englishman staying with their new brides at a famous honeymoon hotel. As they retired to bed they agreed that they would get together the next day and exchange experiences over some drinks. Thus it came to pass next day that the German was asked:

"How did you get on last night?"

"Acht, vunce to begin wid, then vunce von hour later, und every time der clock strucken, vunce again, vich vass eight times in eight hour."

"And what did your wife say?"

"Wunderbar, Wunderbar!!"

The Frenchman told them:

"I am straightway on the work. Den I am on the work again when I receive back my breath. Den I sleep and start again, and sleep and start again. Vingt fois, tventy time, them I am halted, finis."

"What did your wife say?"

"Ah, elle dit, Magnifique, encore, magnifique!!"

The Englishman had been very quiet: "Come tell us, how many?"

"Once," he said.

"Once! – what did your wife say at dawn?"

"Get off, we need some sleep."

# KEEPING ABREAST OF THINGS

There was a new African State set up and they wished to set up a legal system as good as that in Great Britain. Accordingly they studied the law reports in various papers and went ahead accordingly. When this new system was in full swing they invited the Lord Chancellor to go and give it the O.K. Accordingly the Lord Chancellor paid a visit, and was much impressed with what he saw. Counsel and Judges wore wigs, English fashion, they had a Jury System, and all was according to the Book. However, he was astonished when he attended his first big case. Before the proceedings opened a Pigmy entered the Court, and proceeded to feel the breasts of the policewomen, the lady shorthand writers, and those of the girls who happened to be in the public gallery. "What's all this about?" he gasped.

"Ah, my Lord, we read the papers from your country, and from time to time we know that 'A little titter runs round the Court', well, that's him."

## THAT'S MY STORY

A male ballet dancer, having Sunday as his day off, went for a walk in the woods. He met a large and ugly toad, who startled him by saying:

"Hey, don't pass me by!"

"What's going on?" enquired the young man.

"I'm a bewitched human being," said the toad, "and if I can find a man who was born on February 29th, which is less than one chance in a thousand, as you know, I can bring him great good luck."

The young man said he was born on February 29th, what did he have to do to acquire the good luck?

"Take me to your bed, let me sleep all night with you, and in the morning you will have a wonderful surprise."

So the young man took the great ugly toad back, smuggled him into his theatrical digs, and took him to bed. Just as the landlady brought in the morning cup of tea, the toad turned into a handsome prince.

*　　*　　*

"Is that the story?" enquired the learned Judge.

"Yes, my Lord, that concludes the case for the defence," replied Counsel.


## LIKE FATHER LIKE . . .

Council houses have thin walls. When this couple got married they stayed the night with his parents, who retired to bed, only to be disturbed by the bumping about in the next room.

"Tell you what," whispered father, "every time they do it, we'll do it?"

This was agreed, and after an hour the honeymooners were off again. Father and mother fell into an exhausted sleep, only to be re-awakened at four in the morning. At six father awoke, listened, and said:

"Stop it, Albert, you're killing your mother."

## HANDLE WITH CARE

A new bride was getting in the taxi to go to the station. Suddenly she cried: "Wait! Mother, I've left my gloves somewhere in the reception, go and find them please."

"Oh my child, you don't need your gloves, take it in your bare hand, the same as I did with your father."


## DIZZY HEIGHTS

A man went to join the army, and was sent before the Medical Board. The doctor examined him in the buff, and then instantly sent out for his students: "Look gentlemen," he said, "the biggest one I've ever seen, and I've been an army doctor twenty years." The students looked with awe, and one said: "Sir, can I ask this recruit a question?"

"By all means, go ahead."

"Right, now pardon me Smith, but you appear to have the biggest one of any army recruit, tell me, what is it like when it's down?"

"It's down now," was the reply.

"Good lord! Then tell us, what is it like when it's up?"

"I'm sorry, I don't know, I've never seen it erect, doctor."

"Do you mean to say that a man as well blessed as you is actually impotent? Bad luck that."

"I didn't say that," protested the soldier, "I said I'd never SEEN it up. You see, I've only got enough blood for one of us, and every time he rises, I faint."

## PLEASE LIFT ONLY BY THE HANDLE

By a strange coincidence, two more recruits came in that day with oversize members. They were brothers, and the doctors, unable to believe their eyes, decided to write the matter up in the medical press. Says the head medico, getting out his writing pad: "How do you account for this?"

"It's hereditary, Sir," said the older one.

"Aha" (writing it down) "your father is the cause of these, hey?"

"No, Sir, our mother. It's because of our mother that my brothers and I have such big dicks."

"Your mother! Why you idiot, women don't have them!"

"No, Sir, but she only had one arm, and when it came to getting us in and out of the bath, she had to manage as best she could."

## SATAN REBUKING SIN

A man went to a solicitor and said he must have a divorce.

"Why?" said the man of law.

"Because of my wife's filthy habits."

"What filthy habits?"

"Ooh, I couldn't tell you."

The solicitor explained that if the man wouldn't detail the dirty habits of his wife, there could be no possibility of a divorce.

At last the man blurted it out:

"The fact is," he said, "that every time I go to piss in the sink, I always find it full of dirty washing-up."

# A SCABBY TRICK

There was a girl who went to a priest to confess that she had been "naughty" with a man. She said it was her first experience, and she was certainly a bit vague about it.

"Look here, daughter," said the priest, undoing her blouse, "did he do this?" – "Yes Father." (Having a right good maul.) "Did he do this?"

"Yes, Father."

The priest took her knickers off. . . . "Did he do this?" – "Yes he did."

Shortly she was on her back and the priest's trousers open. . . . "Did he do this?" "Yes, indeed Father."

After the job was fully completed and they were both doing up their clothes, the priest says: "Well, you've told me everything, you can have absolution."

"But, Father, he did something else."

"Something else?" (His mind visualised several unpleasant ideas.)

"Yes, he gave me the pox!"

# SECOND CHILDHOOD

A little girl was in the park crying when a respectable old gentleman asked her why. She said: "I want one of those things like my brother's got, that sticks out, and then lays down, and then sticks out again."

The respectable old gentleman began to cry too.

# DESERT ISLAND DISHED

There was a man who was overweight, and this worried him, so he went to his doctor. The doctor said: "I can put you right, but it's rather pricey; take these pills, one each night, and come back in two weeks."

The man returned in a fortnight looking fine. "Tell me?" said the doctor.

"Well, Sir, every night when I went to bed, I dreamed that I was in a harem with twenty of the most voluptuous randy girls, and I had to lay all of them. It was marvellous, and I've lost a stone in weight!"

"That'll be twenty quid," said the doctor.

"And well worth it," said the patient.

Now this patient had an acquaintance, a mean miserable beggar, who was also too fat, so he sent him for the same treatment.

When this miser reported back to the doctor, he too had lost a stone, but he wasn't in the least grateful.

"Look here," he said, "I dreamed I was on a desert island, and every night a huge Blackamoor came out with a long sharp knife; he chased me round and round 'til dawn, swearing he would castrate me. I used to wake up sweating and half dead. . . ."

"But you lost a stone!"

"Yes, but my mate had girls with big. . . ."

"That's your fault. You *would* have yours on the National Health."


# AN ODD ONE

An Irishwoman went to the Marriage Guidance clinic to ask about a divorce:

"Does your husband ill-treat you?" – "No, he's a kind, gentle, man."

"Does he drink and gamble?" – "No, he gives me all his money."

"Then of course, unfaithfulness must be the trouble?"

"Yes, I suppose it must be, one of the kids isn't his."

# UNITED WE STAND

There had been some massive take-over bids in the Insurance world, and four of Britain's largest companies had amalgamated. They built a new headquarters in the Strand which was truly marvellous. The Planning Authority had insisted that it be finished off with a giant piece of sculpture, as is the modern custom, and this was the problem.

The Directors met, and as money was no object, they decided to engage Einstein. It was written into the contract that the sculpture was not to be "modern", but it was to be a true representation of the amalgamation of four great Insurance companies, no more, no less. In return, Einstein asked that the plinth be close-boarded and the thing kept under drapes until finished, which was readily agreed.

\*   \*   \*

When the day of unveiling came, all were there in their toppers, Directors, MPs, and distinguished men as well. The ladies included some of the noblest in the land, with their daughters.

When the Lord Mayor of London pulled the string, a shocking sight was disclosed. The thing was no more than a huge shield divided into four quarters, and in each quarter a naked couple, larger than life, manifestly having intercourse. The Chairman was livid! "We demand an explanation," he shouted, "and it had better be a good one, or you'll never see a penny of that twenty thousand quid!"

Einstein remained calm: "Gentlemen," he said, "I have fulfilled my instructions. Observe in the first quarter an Actuary in a whore's parlour – that is *Commercial Union*. In the second quarter a Director is having his typist across the desk, which is surely *Employers' Liability*. Next we have a Banker's son with his fiancée in an hotel, that's *Mutual Trust*. The last couple are clearly married to each other, which is *Wesleyan and General*." (*They had to pay him the money*.)

# RISING TO THE OCCASION

There was a young man who considered himself sex starved. He was randy all the time. He was dying to join a nudist camp, and finally, after a good deal of wangling, got himself invited to a Club, "on probation".

His friend told him what to do. You prove your identity at the gate, then they let you into the hut, and you strip off. Then you walk down a glade, and the Secretary will meet you and introduce you.

"Remember!" he said, "behave yourself, it's all very respectable."

The man swore to be good, and all went according to plan. He left the hut, walked down the path, and spotted a young woman with splendid breasts, a round full bottom, a shaved quim, in fact, the lot.

"Excuse me," he said, "but I'm looking for the Secretary."

"I'm the Secretary."

"Oh indeed, then I'm very glad to meet you."

"Yes, I can see that you are."

# HE WASN'T A LABOUR MAN

A midwife on her day off called in the hospital for her wages. At that moment the phone rang, and there was a mild panic. It seemed that yet another emergency case had arisen, and no one to take it. The off-duty midwife must go.

"But I'm in civvies."

"That doesn't matter."

"My car's in dock."

"We'll get you a taxi."

All this took time, and as soon as the taxi arrived, the nurse flung herself into it, and said: "For Pete's sake hurry up, the baby's due in ten minutes."

The taxi driver stopped, opened the door, and said: "Oh no yer don't Missus, not in my cab yer don't."

# WISSED IN THE POTTLE

A working-class woman was up before the Beak for assaulting her neighbour on the bus.

"I don't understand it," he said, "you and Mrs Maggs have been neighbours and friends for years, how did this fight start?"

"It was like this, your Worship. I'm on the bus going with me sample to the doctor's see, and Mrs Bloggs gets on, see. . . ."

"Yes yes, get on with it, what happened?"

"Well she asts me 'What have yer got in that bottle?' and I replies 'Piss' and she says, 'Oh it's piss to me is it?' in that case, 'Shit to you too', and that's how it all started."

# LOOKING GLASS

A working-class woman was very jealous because all her neighbours were getting things free off the National Health. One had new teeth, another had new glasses, and when the woman next door got a free hearing aid, it was the last straw.

She went to the doctor and said: "I want something free on the National Health as well."

"Oh indeed," said the doctor, humouring her, "and what do you fancy, eh?"

"Well, Doctor, I fancy I'd like you to cut a hole in my stomach."

The doctor thought he could see what was coming, "Ah, I see, your husband is not satisfied with the one you've got, and you want me to make you a new one?"

"Oh no, certainly not, I want you to make the hole and fit a piece of glass in it."

"Look here, Mrs Shufflebottam, I'm a busy man, I'll prescribe some tranquillisers, and please send the next patient in."

"I don't fancy tranquillisers!"

"Well, what do you fancy then?"

"I've just told you – a womb with a view!"

# CHEESED OFF

Two rough types were employed as Night Soil men, and one very hot summer day they were approaching their cart, each with a full bucket, when a local factory hooter blew for dinner-hour. They put down their burdens, and each produced a packet of sandwiches, which they proceeded to eat at the roadside. The stench was noisesome, blowflies filled the air, and passers-by crossed the road.

"Hey Dan," said Bill, "it stinks enough now, without you stirring it round with your arm!"

"Stirring it up? Don't be bloody silly, I've dropped me bread and cheese."

# MOVING STORY

A Chinaman went to the doctor because he was very constipated, and the doctor gave him a prescription for a good stiff dose of "number nines".

"Come back in three days, and tell me how you get on."

Three days later the Chinaman was back.

"Have you moved yet?"

"No, Slir, me no moovee not at all."

The doctor gave him a double dose, and awaited results.

Three days later, still no results, so the quack gave him the stiffest possible dose of the very strongest purgative, and said: "Come back in three days, without fail."

When the man came back:

"Have you moved yet?"

"No, Slir, me no moovee yet, me moovee tomorrow, house full of slit."

# BELLY LIKELY

Sherlock Holmes went up to Heaven. Saint Peter said: "What's your claim?"

"I claim to be the world's greatest detective," said Holmes.

"Pass a test, and you can stay in Heaven," said Peter.

"What test?"

"There are millions of people in here. If you can pick out Adam and Eve, you win."

(Holmes had no difficulty, they were the only two without navels!)

# APPEASEMENT

There was a doctor who had a working-class National Health practice, and, just before going on holiday he was explaining the business to a young locum.

"There is one man," he said, "an Irishman, and a proper pest – never satisfied." At this moment the doctor looked out of the window, and added: "Ah, he is coming in now."

The trouble-maker came into the surgery, and started shouting that his wife was having too many kids, why didn't the doctor do something about it?

"Ah yes, I could put your wife on the Pill."

The man protested that Father O'Flynn would never allow it.

"Then why don't *you* do something about it, wear a sheath."

"Damn that for a game – like eating a toffee with the paper on."

After a lot more argument the man shouted that the doctor must put matters right, or he would write to the Medical Council about it.

"Oh very well, very well," said the doctor, "I'll write a prescription; now clear off, I'm busy."

The man set off and found a chemists shop. The chemist broke the seal, read the prescription, and said: "I want none of your funny jokes here, take it to a greengrocer."

As surgery was finishing the Irishman came back. "What the blazes is the meaning of this!" he yelled, flourishing the piece of paper under the doctor's nose. . . . "Half a pound of dried peas, one to be placed in the left shoe each morning."

"It will make you limp all the time," said the doctor.

## BACK TO *SKOLL*!

A stranger at a nudist camp had drunk too much tea. He was having a real good pee behind a bush before he saw a nice girl doing the same. Neither could stop, and to cover her embarrassment the girl said:

"Good health, here's to you, and PLEASE don't tell anybody about this."

"That's a bargain," said he, "provided we touch glasses!"

"Agreed," she said, "kiss my quim."

"That's not at all what you promised," he protested.

"Oh yes it is, you will be putting your old mug against my little cup."

## WET BLANKET

A well brought up girl went to a dance, missed the last bus, and had to walk home. She lost her way, and finished up sleeping on the porch of a synagogue.

Her mother, when she heard the story, was a little bit upset. "It was such a damp night, I only hope you're going to be all right after the experience."

The girl said she was quite all right. A few months later she was obviously pregnant.

Her mother said: "You didn't tell the truth did you, about where you slept that night?"

"Oh yes I did, Mother, but I forgot to mention that when I woke up in the morning I found a little *dew* on me."

## TO HER CREDIT

A man got in touch with a girl through a Marriage Bureau. He rather liked her, but he told the Bureau Manager that he wouldn't consider marriage without a trial of her sexual abilities. "We businessmen never purchase in bulk without a sample," he added.

The girl, when she heard about this, sent back the answer: "I too am business trained, and I don't have to give free samples, but I can, and will give bankers' and solicitors' references."

## ANSWER TO PRAYER

A Minister heard that in his rather superior parish the harmless little parties that went on were really orgies. He wangled himself an invite to such a party, and it started off with harmless games and background music.

However, after the drinks had gone round a few times, more and more people began to undress, and everybody was mauling everybody else. The Minister retired to a bedroom to pray furiously.

He had not been there very long when a smashing girl walked in, stark naked. "Do you want me?" he said.

"Not particularly, but I drew you in the raffle."

## NUTS TO THAT

A Women's Army Corps officer during the war thought that her girls were getting frustrated. When a Yankee Division straight from the line moved into the next town she saw her chance, and rang up the Commanding Officer.

"Would you like to come and take dinner with me and escort me to the dance afterwards?"

"Deelighted, Marm."

"Could you bring along some enlisted men for the girls?"

"I should tell you, Marm, my privates are black."

"That's all right I can give you a bath before dinner, but can you bring along some enlisted men?"

## WHAT A WET

Some toffee-nosed WRENS ran a dance, and, for want of better, sent along some tickets to the Naval barracks. The WREN C.O. was a bit worried about things, and decided to station herself at the ticket desk to see who came in.

The first to arrive was a rough Portsmouth petty officer, he said:

"Before I go in, where's the piss-corner?"

"My good man, proceed right down the corridor until you see a door on your left marked 'Gentlemen Only'. Take no notice of that, just walk right in."

## ENLARGEMENT

A young married man took his wife to an overworked National Health doctor to be examined, because he thought she might be pregnant, as she had missed one month.

The doctor took up a rubber stamp, made a tiny imprint on the woman's belly, and dismissed them, calling for the next patient.

The husband, overcome with curiosity undressed the wife as soon as they got home, and got a powerful magnifying glass to work. He read:

"As soon as you can read this in ordinary daylight, without glasses, it's time to bring her back."

There was a young curate named Borrow
Who eloped with two nuns, to his sorrow,
They lived on an isthmus
And one he called Christmas
The other he christened Tomorrow.

"You need exercise man, and fresh air!"
Said the doctor, to Sinjohn Sinclair.
To her joy and surprise
He forced his wife's thighs —
The "exercise" brought a fresh heir!

The learned Lord Chancellor Veres
Suspended a shocked House of Peers
And to Coventry hied
For Godiva's great ride,
As he'd not seen a white horse for years.

There was a yachtswoman of Hale
Who had a leak under the rail,
A caulker named Goat
Put a plug in her boat,
And now she's a ship in full sail.

"My bride was no virgin," said Braining,
"I've never received such a draining!
Mere up and down thrust
Could be natural lust,
But side-to-side action, that's training!"

The boys are back together again!

AUF WIEDERSEHEN Pet.

TWO

## by Fred Taylor

Now available: the second novel based on the hugely popular
series by Dick Clement and Ian La Frenais, probably the best
script-writing team in Britain today.

In response to an SOS from Barry, our heroes reassemble –
more than two years since their fond farewell on a building-
site in Germany.

This time the scene is Spain's notorious Costa del Crime and
Dennis, Neville, Oz, Barry, Wayne, Moxy and Bomber, still
chronically short of cash and hungry for travel, adventure and
mayhem, rebound from crisis to hilarious crisis.

They and their long-suffering wives and sweethearts find
themselves involved in scrapes that make the old days in
Dusseldorf seem like a dream cruise on the Rhine . . .

HUMOUR/TV TIE-IN   0 7221 36749   £2.75

*The dreadful carnage continues . . .*

# Witches

## 7: THE FEUD

### The chilling horror series by
### *JAMES DARKE*

John Ferris, the hero of James Darke's spine-tingling horror books, has suffered grievously from the ministrations of those evil men and women who worship the Black Arts. But they are still on his trail.

Not many leagues distant, in cellars that reeked of monkshood, henbane and thorn-apple, dark-garbed figures with arcane names were pursuing their gruesome rites by the sinister light of black candles. And before long even the watchful Ferris would be lured into their midst, and find himself as helpless as a new-born babe in the face of their fiendish magic . . .

·HORROR      0 7221 5201 9      £1.95

Don't miss:
THE PRISONER           THE MEETING
THE TRIAL              THE KILLING
THE TORTURE            THE PLAGUE
THE ESCAPE

*EVERYTHING YOU NEED TO KNOW ABOUT SPORT
(AND A LOT OF THINGS YOU DON'T)!*

# The Book Of

# SPORTS
## LISTS

## CRAIG AND DAVID BROWN

Who 'floats like a butterfly and stings like one too'?
Who gave up sex for a year in order to improve his game
– and what does it cost to persuade John McEnroe to
play with your racquets for a year? Which sportsman
said 'I'd give my right arm to be a pianist' – and what do
Torvill and Dean have to say about each other?

THE BOOK OF SPORTS LISTS brings together the
most remarkable things ever done and the funniest
things ever said in the name of sport around the world.
Record-breakers and blunderers, prudes and Casanovas,
good sports and bad sports, they're all in THE BOOK OF
SPORTS LISTS.

**NON-FICTION/HUMOUR/SPORT     0 7221 1935 6     £2.50**

*Don't miss Craig Brown and Lesley Cunliffe's THE
BOOK OF ROYAL LISTS, also available in Sphere
Books.*

Get on yer bike!

**Goods On Board**

The hilarious new novel by
**SIMON MAYLE**

Dear Reader,

I promise you that this book is so witty you'll be reading it
aloud to the nearest traffic warden. You'll need three boxes of
extra-strong hankies for the sad bits. You'll find brilliant new
insights into modern romance.

Besides all this, there's a load of great stuff about motor-
cycling, Life, and what it's like to wear leather.

Basically, reading this is nearly as good as doing a ton down
the South Circular, or a wheelie along the Mall. Go for it!

James

0 7221 5750 9   GENERAL FICTION   £2.50

*ALL IS REVEALED . . .*

# HENRY ROOT'S

## A-Z of Women

### 'The Definitive Guide'

*I know what you're thinking. You're thinking: Women, eh? What's there to say about women? The bedroom and the kitchen. The duvet and the blender. The corset and the rubber glove. That covers it, you're thinking. But Root on women, that's different… that's very different indeed.*

*So to balance the current spate of books by women on men, the incomparable Henry Root has gone out in the field and up at the sharp end – and has come back with the ultimate guide to women today.*

**0 7221 3067 8   Humour   £2.50**

# A selection of bestsellers from SPHERE

**FICTION**

| | | |
|---|---|---|
| FAMILY ALBUM | Danielle Steel | £2.95 ☐ |
| SEVEN STEPS TO TREASON | Michael Hartland | £2.50 ☐ |
| DUNN'S CONUNDRUM | Stan Lee | £2.95 ☐ |
| GOLDEN TALLY | Pamela Oldfield | £2.95 ☐ |

**FILM AND TV TIE-IN**

| | | |
|---|---|---|
| BOON | Anthony Masters | £2.50 ☐ |
| AUF WIEDERSEHEN PET 2 | Fred Taylor | £2.75 ☐ |
| LADY JANE | Anthony Smith | £1.95 ☐ |

**NON-FICTION**

| | | |
|---|---|---|
| HENRY ROOT'S A-Z OF WOMEN | Willie Donaldson | £2.50 ☐ |
| THE FALL OF SAIGON | David Butler | £3.95 ☐ |
| LET'S FACE IT | Christine Piff | £2.50 ☑ |
| A QUIET YEAR | Derek Tangye | £2.25 ☐ |

*All Sphere books are available at your local bookshop or newsagent, or can be ordered direct from the publisher. Just tick the titles you want and fill in the form below.*

Name _____

Address _____

_____

*Write to Sphere Books, Cash Sales Department, P.O. Box 11, Falmouth, Cornwall TR10 9EN.*

*Please enclose a cheque or postal order to the value of the cover price plus:*

*UK: 55p for the first book, 22p for the second book and 14p for each additional book ordered to a maximum charge of £1.75.*

*OVERSEAS: £1.00 for the first book plus 25p per copy for each additional book.*

*BFPO & EIRE: 55p for the first book, 22p for the second book plus 14p per copy for the next 7 books, thereafter 8 p per book.*

*Sphere Books reserve the right to show new retail prices on covers which may differ from those previously advertised in the text or elsewhere, and to increase postal rates in accordance with the PO.*